Clarissa Barton 1.95

By Evelyn King Mumaw

HERALD PRESS, SCOTTDALE, PENNSYLVANIA

WOMAN ALONE


Library of Congress Catalog Card Number: 72-109937
International Standard Book Number: 0-8361-1620-8
Printed in the United States

Front cover design by Mary Lou Brubaker
Book Designed by Jan Gleysteen

*Dedicated to the*
*Single Women Graduates*
*of Eastern Mennonite College,*
*Harrisonburg, Virginia,*
*many of whom are demonstrating*
*wholesome single living.*

# FOREWORD

Early in my years of college personnel work at Eastern Mennonite College it became apparent to me that a significant percentage of college women would likely not marry until late in life or not at all. And yet the general emphasis on campus was on preparing women for marriage with almost no recognition of the need to prepare them to live well while they were unmarried. This appeared to me to be a very damaging situation.

Cautiously, but certainly, I began to talk, to write, to study, and to do research regarding single women. In 1951 I wrote a thesis for my master's degree called *A Study of the Status of the Unmarried Women Graduates of Eastern Mennonite College*. This study has served as background material for lectures and counseling since then. But the requests for written material for single women have come frequently and persistently. So I have written *Woman Alone*.

Having worked with these materials over a period of at least fifteen years, I find it impossible at some points to know whether someone else's thoughts have become mine through much rumination or whether the thoughts were mine independently and I found them voiced later in someone else's writings. I have meant to be fair in giving credit to written works.

My greatest debt of recognition is to the many women who have shared with me openly through the years and especially to those who have refused to allow me to drop the idea of writing.

My husband John deserves special appreciation. He wholeheartedly stood by me in this project, which speaks to interests and concerns he has had as a pastor for many years.

# CONTENTS

# 1

## Where's Your Daddy?

I had lived in my second-floor apartment only a short time before I heard the door at the foot of the stairway open gently. Then I heard the sound of little feet hesitantly coming up the stairs. When I peeked around the corner my eyes met the inquisitive brown eyes of four-year-old Beth who was evidently on one of her get-acquainted tours of the friendly neighborhood. I invited her in. She moved unobtrusively from room to room of the four-room apartment and then settled down beside me on the sofa to get acquainted. Suddenly she looked up into my face and inquired, "Where's your daddy?"

Since I was ten or fifteen years older than her mother, I was certain that I understood the meaning of her question. "I don't have a daddy, Beth," I replied.

This book is written for women who, in Beth's terms, do not have a "daddy." Over a period of fifteen or more years, I have been asked repeatedly to write the ideas which I have shared in counseling, in classes, in conversations, in group discussions, and in addresses about living well as single women. I am ready now to look at various phases of this life situation.

Even as I begin to write I know that you, my single women readers, will have a great variety of reactions to what I have to share. A few of you will disagree with me violently and wonder where I got my wild ideas. On the same points some others of you will think I'm really "on the beam."

You see, you are quite a diverse group of women. Although you have the common denominator of being unmarried, your reactions to this state and to your experiences evolving from it are of almost infinite variety. So please remember that your attitudes and experiences are not necessarily the norm for all single women.

I am writing especially for *Christian* single women, that is, for women who have experienced spiritual birth through faith in Jesus Christ. I assume you are interested in living your lives under the lordship of Christ regardless of your marriage status.

# 2

## Why Aren't You Married?

My roly-poly three-year-old nephew was lolling on my lap and exercising his expanding vocabulary and philosophic bent.

"Mommy's married."

"Umhuh."

"And Bobby's mommy is married."

"Umhuh."

"But — you're not married!"

I started to chuckle because I could already read in his big brown eyes the question that was forming.

"Why aren'tcha married?"

This question comes sooner or later and it may come many times. If no one has asked you directly why you are not married, you have likely asked it of yourself repeatedly.

Why do so many women remain unmarried? Frequently the real reasons and the felt reasons are not the same. Let's take a look at some of the possible reasons for women remaining single.

## *There must be something the matter with me!*

Doris sobbed bitterly as she squirmed in her chair. "Miss King, what is the matter with me? I just never date around here!"

She was candid enough to say what many women feel and never have the courage to express. Their lack of dating and failure to marry make them feel that they are seriously lacking in some important qualification for marriage. They become certain that there really is something very much the matter with them.

This is not always a wrong judgment. However, you should compare a cross section of women who have married with a comparative group of women who have not married. You will be amazed at the number of women who have "something the matter with them" who have married and the number who apparently do not have "something the matter with them" who have not married!

Doris, for instance, was a pleasant, intelligent, friendly, well-dressed, healthy young woman in her early twenties with potential for making a good companion, mother, and homemaker. Her qualities for contributing positively to marriage far exceeded those of many of her peers who were dating or were already married.

It is good to evaluate yourself occasionally, not just for marriageability but for general acceptability in the cultural-social-religious group with which you have identified. Think in terms of attitudes, disposition, manner, appearance, relationships, and quality of living. Note your weaker areas and set about to deal with these constructively. But unless you become aware of some very glaring fault or lack in yourself, be very slow to credit your singleness to having "something the matter" with you.

## *I can't find anyone who meets my ideal.*

A measure of idealism in choosing a husband is very important. And women had far better remain single than to be unhappily married. I've known many women who have turned away from friendships and offers of marriage and moved on alone rather than become involved in a partnership they felt had too many risks in it. I admire these women for taking that position in the face of strong social pressure to marry. I wish many others would have had enough insight and courage to do the same.

But there is another side to this. You may be very unrealistic in your perfectionistic approach to choosing a husband. Men do not come in perfect packages, you know, just as women do not. Maybe you are expecting a great deal more from a husband than you have to offer as a wife. And maybe you are holding out for qualifications that really are not very significant for a successful marriage. Check your "ideal man" and see if some of the features you are requiring may not really be quite superficial and unimportant.

And if you are making the claim that you cannot find a man who meets your ideal, please be certain that you are being completely honest. Be sure you are not using this claim as an alibi to boost your own ego and image while you cover deep inside of you the real reasons.

If you are being honest with yourself and if you have gotten your requirements for a husband down to a realistic minimum and there is still no one who "fills the bill," then I am all for your remaining single.

## *There just aren't enough men to go around!*

You are absolutely right! I have read many figures comparing the number of marriageable men and women in our country. While these figures vary a great deal, they almost all indicate that there are several million more unmarried women than men. (This is another reason why women should be slow to judge themselves as not being desirable for marriage.)

In addition to the fact that there are many more unmarried women than men, there is the tendency for clustering of unmarrieds of either sex in disparate areas. Vocational opportunities and living conditions account for this difference. So if you are employed in an office or schoolroom or hospital in a large city, you are likely just one more of the great number of unmarried women in that area. There may be concentrations of men in industry nearby, but the chances are that your interests and theirs are so different that you seldom meet and if you do, you find common ground for building friendships rather limited.

This numerical inequality of eligible men and women is also an intensified problem to women in upper levels of higher education.

Marg was a college junior. Her charming, black eyes snapped with a sort of frustrated anger. "I just dread to go home! Back there I dated all the time and so they all think I should be about ready to get married and here I am — not even dating!"

I pulled out a copy of her class register and suggested we look at the men's list. The class was small enough that we knew casually most of its members. We noted the number of fellows who were already married when they came to college as compared to the women who were married when they came as freshmen. We also noted the number of fellows who had steadies back home or in other communities as compared with women who had non-campus steadies. Slowly it began to dawn on Marg that the inequality of numbers of eligible men and women on the campus was enormous. So I quietly, but emphatically, suggested to her, "Just tell those people back home that there simply are not enough nice guys to go around!"

## *My responsibilities will not permit marriage.*

Edna feels that she should take care of her invalid mother and blind father as long as they need her. Being in their own home means so much to them that she feels responsible to make it possible for them to stay there.

Joyce has assumed the care and support of her retarded brother; there just was no one else to do it and she could not consent to having him placed in a large, impersonal state institution.

Martha took over the responsibilities of care for the home and her younger brothers and sisters when her mother died and now it seems the family just assumes she will always be there.

Oftentimes women in circumstances like these have little opportunity to associate closely with men and when they do they quickly become uncomfortable because of the conflict of personal loyalties with normal desires. So in a very real way their responsibilities lessen their likelihood of marriage.

## *My handicap has ruled out marriage for me.*

Congenital defects, crippling due to accidental injury, and various diseases are among the physical handicaps canceling out the possibility of marriage for many women. It is amazing how many blind, deaf, crippled, or ill women have married, but even so, these have been limiting factors which have deferred or canceled out marriage for many other women.

## *I just can't make it.*

Anne shook her head solemnly. "I just can't make it. You know, I'm beginning to believe that I never will be able to marry. I get so far but when the man gets serious and ready for marriage I get frightened out of my wits and I just can't go on! Maybe if the really right man would come along I'd feel differently, but I don't know. I'm just scared of it. I don't think I could make a go of it!"

Anne is far from being alone in these reactions. Fear and insecurity keep many women from venturing into marriage. Usually these fears have their roots in childhood experiences and cannot be shaken easily. A woman who desires marriage but is kept from it by fear and feelings of inadequacy may be able to work through these conflicts with the help of a well-trained counselor.

## *"I choose to remain unmarried."*

Here and there you find them — the women who have become so absorbed in a profession or way of life that seems to be incompatible with marriage that they have chosen to give themselves to their vocation rather than to marriage.

Ruth was thirty-five, poised, gracious, and very gifted. I listened for her response when an acquaintance questioned her about her attitude toward marriage. She lifted her head a bit and spoke with quiet certainty. "When I made my decision to earn my doctorate, I also decided simultaneously to remain single and devote my life to professional interests. I believe that it is in this way that I can be of the greatest service to God and my fellowmen."

Among Christian women who have chosen to remain unmarried are those persons who have a clear sense of divine calling to a work that requires singlehood. They have chosen to follow and remain in this leading even though they were aware that this choice was also most likely the choice to remain unmarried.

# 3

## So What! What Difference Does It Make?

Tall girls have one set of problems. Left-handed people have another set. Widows have still another set. Teenagers are beset by their peculiar problems. Aged people have another type of problem. Married people have a great many problems. And, of course, single women have problems, too. In fact, every reasonably distinct group of persons has its own particular set of problems to work through. Life is a continuous problem-solving experience for everyone. So when we talk about the problems of unmarried women, this does not for a moment bring you into focus as strange persons. Actually you would be very strange indeed and different from the rest of mankind if you did not have problems.

I was talking with several single professional women in an isolated area of another country. Since I had heard much from other sources regarding difficulties encountered by single women in isolated locations in foreign cultures, I raised a question about the matter.

One middle-aged woman stiffened immediately. "We are persons!" she exclaimed. "We are not different from married women. I just don't see any point in talking about single women's problems!"

I did not pursue my question at all in the face of this rebuff; I simply wondered what problems my friend was so vigorously trying to deny. I wondered this because I had to weigh her testimony against dozens of testimonies that there are complex problems.

So when I ask what difference it makes that you are not married, I know that it does make some difference. While you need to find answers to many of the same problems that your married sisters have to cope with, you also have another set of problems to resolve. Furthermore, your individual set of problems will vary somewhat from those of your single friends due to difference in personality, family relationships, church affiliation, geographical location, and many other less tangible factors.

Many of the single women's problems emerge from attitudes in the society they belong to and from the cultural practices of that society.

We need to recognize some of these attitudes and practices as we try to understand the problems they create.

## *You belong to a minority group.*

Even though there may be several million unmarried women in our country, they are so scattered that in almost every community they are in the minority. It seems that usually minorities have to contend with pressures from the majority.

Minority groups are often stereotyped. Single women are no exception. Terms like old maid, spinster, and maiden lady are likely to conjure up the stereotype of a gaunt, quaintly dressed, middle-aged woman looking out over the top of her glasses while she spits out some sharp meddling remark or makes some horrified, naive expression about sex. While these terms are gradually being replaced by more contemporary expressions such as bachelor girls, and these quaint images are giving way to the image of rather sophisticated or glamorous career women, the old stereotype persists to a marked degree. If you doubt that, watch the billboards and other advertising media for a while.

Dr. M. D. Hugen noted from his research that the stereotype of the single woman has undergone extensive revisions at various times in America's history and that each change has come when society's concept of the marriageable woman has changed. For instance, when pioneer days and wilderness living called for strong women with determination and character, the single woman's image was that of a mild person who kept mild-mannered cats and took care of her nieces. More recently when the emphases of psychology became dominant the marriageable woman was said to be attractive, personable, psychically mature, and well developed, and the single woman was stereotyped as homely, frustrated, maladjusted, and neurotic. [1]

Stereotypes are seldom, if ever, kind or fair. The stereotype of the single woman is no exception. Various researchers have declared that there is no one type of personality that is characteristic of single women. There are among them those who are noted for their charm and beauty as well as those who are conspicuously lacking in these traits. Some are retiring and some are aggressive. Some of them are selfish and egocentric, while others are generous and unselfish.

And yet in many parts of the country stereotypes of single women persist. The women in these areas often receive the kind of treatment that indicates a widespread acceptance of the stereotype.

Minority groups are often a favorite subject

1. M. D. Hugen, *The Church's Ministry to the Older Unmarried* (Grand Rapids: Wm. B. Eerdmans Publishing Company, 1959), p. 35.

of ridicule among the majority. Unmarried women have not escaped this sort of attention. It is amazing how many doctors of philosophy and ministers of the gospel who consider themselves much too broad-minded and humane to tell jokes about persons of other races or about handicapped persons, still try to bring down the house by clever "old maid" jokes!

Minority groups are under much pressure to conform to patterns established by the majority. For instance: the majority of people in our social structure exist in couples and social activity involving adult men and women has come to be planned almost entirely for couple participation. In situations where activities are planned with couples in mind, a lone individual tends to become an uneasy problem to manage. What does anyone do with just one person?

A number of years ago I was serving as one of the sponsors of a college class. When a senior banquet was held in a lovely local banquet room, I was invited by the class to join them and was informed that I would be seated with the special guests at the speaker's table. When I arrived at the table, I soon discovered that everyone else there was part of a two-some. Beside me there was an empty chair behind an undesignated table setting. I chuckled inside of myself. "Poor people," I thought, "they just do not know what to do with so strange a phenomenon as a lone person!" I've never quite decided what the psychology of that empty place really was, although I have some ideas about it. I do know the host group was helpless in handling the situation.

You may also have this sort of dilemma to face as you try to find your place in adult social activities.

## *You belong to a society that glamorizes marriage and scorns singleness.*

In general, the American society judges a woman's success or failure in life largely on the basis of marriage. If she has found a husband and changed her title from Miss to Mrs., she has arrived! Society's greatest requirement of her has been met in marriage. She may lack many of the strengths and fine qualities of her single sister. However, because she is married, she will be judged with tolerance, if she need be judged at all.

You, on the other hand, are judged as never having quite arrived. In order for you to have "a place in the sun" you will need to achieve a very high level of excellence in many areas of development and even then there will be many people who judge you as having failed in life if you move toward forty and on toward the close of life without having married.

Oh, most people have not really stated this

attitude specifically, but they have implied it over and over again.

Parents often imply that marriage is success and singlehood is failure. From little up their daughters are groomed for the wedding day. Family conversations refer to the time when they will be married. Conversation assumes that it is a settled fact that they will marry. And if the teens roll by and a daughter still has not married, she is subtly but surely made aware that her parents are uneasy about her. Or if a younger daughter marries before an older daughter, the latter senses, either directly or indirectly, from her family that her younger sister has achieved and so far she has failed.

The commercial world picks up this attitude in our society and has a "heyday" with it! Notice how often the advertisements for almost any item a woman could use or might desire designate the item as something that will contribute to her ability to catch a man and marshal him to the altar! "If you are in the pitiful state of being unmarried and you haven't tried our lotion, our exotic meat dish, or our course in grooming, there is still hope for you! You may yet succeed if you will only allow us to help you!" The ads scream at you continuously.

Teenagers take their cue from all of this very early and the panic is on for many girls until they feel certain they have captured their man.

To belong to a peer group with this attitude of urgency and then fail to make the grade is such an intensely humiliating experience that some young women almost or altogether break apart under the stress of it.

When a newly married couple begins housekeeping, friends and relatives usually give lavishly to help them get established in their home. When a single woman establishes her own residence, it is very unlikely that anyone will think in terms of arranging a shower for her or of assisting her by other means.

And so the illustrations from everyday life could be multiplied many times over to show the contrast in our society's attitude toward marriage and singleness.

## *Mature status for you is often deferred or refused.*

Thirty-year-old Mary took her four-year-old neighbor Patsy along to the church picnic. It was time for the potluck food to be arranged on the tables; so the master of ceremonies called, "We would like for the women to please bring the food to the tables."

Mary responded at once. Patsy looked at her with a mixture of surprise and indignation. "Why, you're a girl; you're not a woman!" she exclaimed. The implication? Only married females are women!

Such an idea in a preschooler is not too surprising. But Patsy has a lot of company among adults who quite consistently speak of single women of almost any age as "the girls" and of their married sisters as "the women."

Perhaps the greatest guilt for deferring mature status upon single women lies at the feet of their parents. A single daughter who remains in the home is seldom permitted to function as an adult at the same age her married sister is granted that right. Long after the married sister is running her own household and raising a family and being her husband's bulwark of strength, the single woman is subjected to juvenile requirements. While her parents observe the accomplishments of the married daughter with pride, the single sister of comparative age is being reminded to wear her boots, carry her umbrella, and be ready for dinner on time. The parents are apprehensive about her travel plans and bank account. They question her wardrobe choices and social activities.

Some of this may be justified by the fact that the husband of the married daughter has gained the parents' confidence in assuming responsibility for her. The single daughter is alone in her decision-making and the parents have no one to whom to transfer their sense of responsibility. But even so in many families the fact remains that in all the inconsequential matters affecting the unmarried daughter, she continues to be treated as though she were a very young person long after her married sister is accorded adult status.

It is only fair to mention at this point that not all of the failure to accept single women as mature adults is the fault of the social order surrounding the woman. See if you can think of ways in which you and your friends have invited something less than a mature response from others.

## *The church often considers you a problem.*

It would be wonderful indeed if we could say that these adverse evaluations and the lack of understanding exist only in the secular world and that you need only to relate to the Christian church to find a vastly different atmosphere!

On the basis of study, research, and observation, however, it must be admitted that in much of the Protestant Christian church the prevailing attitudes of the secular culture around us are also the prevailing attitudes in the church. Instead of finding the church a warm, accepting, ministering community, many of you have felt yourself a misfit as part of a minority element. After you no longer belonged with the teenagers there were only the young marrieds to relate to and of course you did not belong in their activities.

If you excelled in teaching or secretarial skills or business ability or art or writing, you found a sort of acceptance. That is, you were very much in demand whenever your skills were needed. And you were glad for this involvement and the privilege to serve in the church, but you found yourself secretly wondering sometimes if you were not being used, if it was not your talent being accepted rather than yourself as a person. For apart from your work involvement the church had little to offer you in your particular status either in preaching, teaching, and counseling or in social activities and fellowship opportunities.

In fact, the church is often one of the strong, though inadvertent, advocates of the idea that marriage is the only honorable state and that to be unmarried borders on the contemptible.

Most of you have sat through sermons or conferences on marriage and the home where these institutions were glamorized and glorified. In the midst of a typical one of these sessions the speaker is likely to say that marriage is God's highest will for woman. You make a mental note that you are outside of God's "highest will" and must be reconciled to never being able to achieve His highest or else must take desperate steps to enter in.

A little later the speaker may inform his congregation that he has heard it said that a single person is one-third a person, a married person is two-thirds a person, and a married person with a child is a whole person! You glance around furtively wondering how many people are thinking about it that you are only a fraction of a person, and you wonder, too, whether you and two other single friends might not add up to almost a whole person.

At the close of the conference some speaker is almost certain to say, "Marriage is the most wonderful experience on earth, but for those who do not marry, God's grace is sufficient." And that is the extent of recognition, understanding, or counsel you have received from the entire program or the church's general program, for that matter.

If the attention of church leaders is called to the number of single women in their congregations and the needs that exist among them, many of them will stand helpless in the face of a social phenomenon they do not understand and are ill-equipped to work with. Others will pass the matter by with a judgmental, "If only these people would accept themselves!"

## *There are personal problems inherent in singleness.*

There are a number of personal problems that have a tendency to go along with being single. They are not the fault of anyone; they just grow out of going it alone. They are not exclusively the problems of single women, but they are often intensified by singleness. They vary greatly in intensity and importance from one woman to another.

Loneliness is one of them. There is in the heart of every ordinary human being the desire for a close, deep, permanent relationship in which two persons can know and be known of each other in every facet of their lives. There is the need within you of having someone to be interested in you and in what you think and do. There is the need within you of having someone to whom you can contribute significantly. There is the need to belong to someone and to have someone belong to you.

Ideally these needs are met most fully in a satisfying marriage relationship. It is also possible for many of these needs to be met in friendships within the same sex. But friendships are often lacking in permanence due to mobility factors and, for many people, to reestablish this sort of relationship over and over becomes increasingly difficult with each new occasion of need. Consequently many single women lack this deep sense of belonging and fellowship. They may have many friends of a more casual level, but because this depth relationship is lacking they carry within themselves a deep well of loneliness.

When a person lacks this significant relationship, life tends to lose its meaning. If nothing you do really has meaning to anyone, why bother? No wonder many single women reach a point in life where they frankly say, "I just don't feel as though life is worth living!" The aches and hurts of this type of lonely existence are excruciating.

I know this is by no means solely the problem of single women. But it does have a tendency to exist with greater frequency among single women. It also becomes more acute as the years roll by and new friendships are formed with less ease. The need of depth friendship is felt more keenly as the exciting adventures of youth lose their appeal. Hence loneliness seems to increase for many women with the passing of time.

The single woman also has biological needs. A woman who marries in the late teens or early twenties and has her sexual needs satisfied regularly may have very little concept of the driving force that might develop within her if she were to be removed for a long period of time from the love relationship with her husband.

But many single women know from long years of single living just how driving and at times exceedingly painful the biological drive for sex fulfillment can become.

Millie was thirty, vivacious, and very much

alive in every way. "Really," she exclaimed emphatically, "I just don't know how to handle the sexual drives and tensions within me. They say you should exercise and get rid of them, but you know how active I am and sometimes I think that just stimulates me. After a strenuous hike I often feel stimulated over my whole body. Sometimes I feel as though I'd go crazy if I didn't get relief! What does a Christian woman do with her drives?"

While this problem like all other problems varies greatly in intensity from woman to woman, there is no question that for many single women unfulfilled sexual cravings create real suffering and conflict. This is often one of the factors which helps to drive women toward deviant sexual behavior. Usually deviant sexual behavior has multiple causes, but since it is generally most easily identified with sexual deprivation we should face frankly some of the perversions into which single women are most frequently ensnared.

When a woman has tremendous emotional capacity to give love, and has very strong sexual drives, but is cut off from almost all heterosexual relationships, she may be very vulnerable and easily led into some form of homosexual relationship. If two such women meet and are drawn together by strong affinity of spirit and interests and find satisfaction in each other's presence and fellowship, it is possible that their pent-up capacity for love in its various forms, which would ordinarily be shared with male partners, may be turned upon each other and before they realize what is happening they may be giving to each other the kind of affection and love expressions that are normally experienced only in intimate heterosexual relationships.

I was concerned about the relationship between Grace and Ellen. They were intelligent gifted women in their early twenties. Both of them had been somewhat socially deprived before coming to college due to geographical location and family background. Now I observed that they were almost always together. When the one spoke of the other, her face lighted up with the love-light one usually sees between boy and girl couples deeply in love. When they spoke to each other it was with the solicitude of a lover. Other students found themselves uncomfortable in their presence.

Both of these women were Christian women, sincere in their commitment to the Lord and to His will for their lives. I became convinced that they had unintentionally gotten into a circumstance they had not planned and did not really understand. They were present in a women's meeting in which I had been asked to discuss social problems of the unmarried. Among these problems I spoke of the "crush" or homosexual relationship. When I observed Grace and Ellen in the audience I hoped that a measure of understanding would come to them through this discussion. But weeks passed by in which the problem became more obvious instead of disappearing. Then one day Grace asked for an appointment to see me.

When she came into my office she quickly broke into sobs. "You know," she finally said, "when we had the women's fellowship meeting in which you talked about improper relationships between two women, I kept trying to tell myself that you were not talking about Ellen and me. But deep in my heart I knew you were! We are in such a mess; we must have help!"

She went on then to tell of the tensions, the guilt, and the spiritual dissipation they were experiencing and the bondage they had become to each other.

This type of problem is found in varying expressions and degrees from pairs of women who engage in demoralizing physical activities with each other's bodies on the one hand to persons who restrain physical expression and yet pour into the relationship the same deep emotional qualities that would ordinarily be found in the heterosexual relationship on the other hand. While these latter relationships sometimes have in them a spiritual quality that seems to enrich the lives of the pair, they also tend to have about them the sort of exclusiveness that repels rather than draws others into their fellowship.

Masturbation is a more common problem. A sort of grimness stole over Erma's face and she looked beyond me into the distance.

"This is the kind of thing one seldom talks about," she said. "But one of the most difficult things I have to deal with as a single person is the problem of masturbation. I can't even remember how or when I started it; I just know that I was quite young, and I guess once you've gotten the habit you always will have to be on guard about it."

After she got past the trauma of disclosure, Erma talked freely of the things that arouse her to sexual desire and the subsequent release by self-stimulation: a sexually exciting story or film, a suggestive song or passionate behavior near at hand, or a realistic sex dream just before waking.

Erma's disclosure represents a frequent difficulty among unmarried women, a difficulty which carries with it feelings of defeat and guilt for most persons who have not been able to control it.

Biological sex urges often drive single women to a desperation for sex experience that leads them into clandestine sexual relationships.

A woman who is plagued persistently with sexual urges and tensions and who finds herself repeatedly thrown into close companionship with a man whom she admires and who becomes increasingly more familiar and affectionate in his behavior toward her may become easy prey for any advances he makes, unless she is very much on guard and has inner strengths to keep her steady under the test.

That many women are succumbing to sexual intercourse outside of marriage is a fact so highly publicized that I need not enlarge on its prevalence. It is a deviant form of behavior snaring many single women.

A real burden for the single woman is carrying the load of life alone. Meg's laugh had a touch of cynicism in it. "I have to laugh deep down inside myself when I hear a husband tell about how wonderful it is to go home to a well-cooked meal in a cozy home where a loving, understanding wife allows him to share his day's activities and relax in her love. He gives the impression that he'd just never make it if it weren't for the wonderful little woman.

"But the same fellow can be awfully intolerant and totally devoid of understanding if the single woman on his committee gets a trifle edgy now and then. It never dawns on him that she is supposed to work in the public all day long just as he does and then go home to an empty house, cook her own meal, and drown out the memories of the day's rub and wear by an exciting book or a round of entertainment. And I'm sure he never stops to consider how well or how ill his lovely little wife might show up under the same conditions!

"I'm not asking for pity — not at all. I'm just asking for common, ordinary understanding, and a sprinkling of patience!"

The heavy load of responsibility that many single women need to carry takes on various forms.

If the single woman has a home of her own, the whole load of management — taxes, bills, maintenance, and repairs — is hers to carry. The same is true of her automobile and any other personal property she possesses.

If she becomes ill, there is likely no one unmistakably responsible to take over her care or to manage her affairs during her illness.

Besides carrying the load of responsibility for her own life, her married brothers and sisters often assume that she is the logical person to care for aging or ailing parents and carry responsibility for them and for their affairs.

# 4

## Can You Take It?

For a good many years I have been listening to and observing what happens to single women as a result of the adverse conditions they encounter both in the secular society and in the church. The responses are as varied as the person involved. Here, too, there is no stereotype.

What are some of the negative undesirable personality traits and qualities which may develop among unmarried women in response to these environmental factors; the dangers that may overtake them in the "dark woods of their personalities"?

Some develop self-hatred. In your formative girlhood years many of you accepted the prevailing attitudes of American culture toward unmarried women. You laughed at old maid jokes, looked down on girls who were not dating, and wondered why in the world attractive neighbor Jane had not gotten married — as though this were certain proof that there must be something radically wrong to account for this state of affairs! You always thought of yourself as a wife and mother when you thought of being an adult. You did not make plans to be a single woman — at least, not for long. Unknowingly but certainly you rejected singleness and most single women. You never really had a basic alteration of attitude. When you reached the mid-twenties and were unmarried, you continued to despise singleness and single women including yourself. And now many of you can identify with the thirty-five-year-old nurse who recently burst out in honest exclamation, "I just hate being an old maid! It's so embarrassing!"

Our culture has continued to reinforce this attitude and although most of the time it is repressed and ignored, it continues to spawn and intensify a whole catalog of damaging feelings. What are some of these?

*Inferiority and worthlessness.* "I must not be of much account. No one wants me. There must be something really the matter with me. What good am I anyhow if no one wants me?"

*Oddity and unattractiveness.* "If I were beautiful — had a smaller nose, brighter eyes, and lovelier teeth — maybe men would fall for me. Or maybe people always notice that I wear size eight shoes and that my figure is very ordinary. I must really be an oddball!"

*Nonacceptance and insecurity.* "No one really likes me. Maybe if I'd go someplace else there would be someone who would really take me in. But where do I go? What can I do? No one really sees my potential and worth."

Out of these and related feelings and attitudes emerge many personality traits and patterns.

Some women withdraw. They have hardly enough courage to face life with its internal and external adverse evaluations. They restrict themselves to their necessary work, to a friend or two very much like themselves, and to a quiet secluded retreat for living.

At times the withdrawal pattern becomes so exaggerated that the person can no longer function as a self-sustaining member of society.

Other women develop the "beat" look. They droop their shoulders and move about with downcast eye as if to say, "Pardon me for living. I just can't help it that I exist."

In search of security some women tie themselves down tightly to routine and ritual and their whole existence may be threatened by the need to make minor changes. They become very rigid. The need to forego a regular prebreakfast cup of coffee, or to sleep in a strange bed, or to change their rising hour, or to lessen the volume of the morning news broadcast — any one of these may be experienced as the major calamity of the day. A change in living arrangements, or a new employer, or a minor change in work assignment may precipitate a serious emotional disturbance.

Others develop an acid disposition. Unadmitted bitterness poisons some women's disposition to the point that it shows itself in facial expression, sharpness of speech, and hostile attitudes toward people and toward God.

Sarcasm is another pattern of reaction to frustration. You probably know unmarried women who are always making gibes at men, couples, mothers, and children. If they can make any or all of these look ridiculous, they've scored a point.

One wing of this group could be called the sour grapes. Listen to them.

"I wouldn't want a man anyhow!"

"I don't have time for men on my schedule!"

"What in the world does she see in him!"

"She can have him if she wants him!"

You may know other single women who have become almost obnoxiously dominant. There is that about them that makes you suspect they are trying to bolster their hurt egos by running the show, dominating the conversation, setting everyone else straight, and having their way.

Then there are the ladies who live in a

dream world. Novels and shows and daydreams about love and sex are their main diet. They try to escape into this never-will-come-true world instead of pouring their energies and vitality into the real world.

A few try to reject their age. You must certainly know a few of the women who are trying to appear young and cute many years after they have left that phase of life behind them. They try frantically to hide the physical changes that indicate aging. They dress like the younger set. They try to attach themselves almost exclusively to persons much younger than themselves, especially to younger women who are still dating occasionally.

Some develop self-pity. These sisters of self-hatred and self-pity have much in common. Perhaps the guise of self-pity is less dense and one can see it for what it is with less effort. Convinced that they have missed life's only and greatest good they become fretful, complaining women who are continually making bids for sympathy or pity. They carry the attitude of "poor me, life has given me a raw deal. It just isn't fair!"

And it appears that when some women do not find a male companion on whom to lavish love, they turn it on themselves in a rather narcissistic way. They treat themselves lavishly to clothing, food, entertainment, and whatever else is luxury to them. They become extremely protective of rights and property, of comfort and ideas.

They are apt to become warped and narrow in their outlook on life so that they see everything from their point of view only. They cannot identify at all with the adolescent, the parent, or the married person. They often become very fussy about little things and minor details take on major significance.

Most of the feelings and personality developments that have been discussed are more or less subtle, hidden, and little understood reactions to remaining unmarried and trying to cope with social dynamics and pressures in the environment.

There are some very overt, specific responses that frequently follow the realization that a woman has likely missed marriage. Sometimes the sudden termination of a friendship that had appeared to be the last likely possibility of marriage will stimulate a violent response.

Sometimes a deadening of womanly characteristics takes place. She was twenty-five, womanly, warm, gracious, and trusting. He was thirty-five, handsome, princely, of high moral character, and of reputable business ability.

When she heard that he had done a lot of serious dating through the years and was usually responsible for terminating these friendships, she was very slow in responding to his interest. She had been deeply hurt in a previous friendship and was determined to be very cautious in this one. But he persisted and finally she trusted him and loved him. When the conquest was certain, he behaved true to pattern and broke the relationship. Now Judy was in the midst of the aftermath.

"I'd like to kill this part of me that wants and wants, and gives and gives, and then suffers and suffers! Why has God made us like this? Why does He allow all this horrible suffering? I'd like to be dead inside so that it can never happen again! I'm going to see if I can crush this part of myself!"

Judy is representative of the women who finally try to nullify their womanly responsiveness to men and develop a hardness or callousness that protects them from further possibilities of involvement and suffering.

Others doubt God's involvement in life. Lois was thirty-five, clever, well-dressed, capable, outgoing, and generous. Usually she was witty and jovial, but today the facade was gone and she was baring her heart in bitterness.

"I'm having a terrible struggle to hold on to my faith! All through our early years we talk about finding God's will for our lives. He is to lead us in vocation, in finding a life companion, and all the rest of it. But here I am — unmarried. I might think the Lord had a hand in it if it were just me, but neither of my sisters are married. You call that the

Lord's leading? It's just that my parents' genes created a group of females that nobody can tolerate! It's a matter of pure chance and I can't find God in it at all!"

The crisis of faith becomes acute for many women in something of the same manner as it did for Lois.

3) Some engage in aggressive man hunting. Convinced by many means that marriage is truly the greatest good, some women in their loneliness will determine to achieve this status at almost any cost. A bachelor or widower coming on the scene becomes their immediate prey. No matter how unsuitable the man may be, a chance is a chance and the chase is on until the poor fellow succumbs or makes his escape!

Many women have gone beyond aggressive husband hunting to the point of deciding that no price is too great to pay in order to experience the love of a man and to discover by involvement what sex is all about. They have been bombarded through various media by the popular current ideas about sex and marriage. Their own strong biological drives for sex fulfillment, plus their psycho-social needs for companionship, have encouraged them to agree with these loose proposals.

4) So for a time they fling aside their Christian principles, tramp on their moral codes, and embrace eagerly a life that burns them to ashes!

# Where Do You Go from Here?

You may be wondering if I think all single women are doomed to gross misunderstandings, warped personalities, fierce loneliness, and illegitimate behavior.

Please do not make hasty conclusions. I invite you to see what the positive, offensive approach to life can hold for the single woman. This means that you will need to deal with your own particular problems and discover the positive, creative ways of living the single life.

## *Develop your understandings.*

To grope around in a mysterious, unknown, uncomprehended milieu contributes to a state of fear, confusion, hopelessness, and frustration. To understand that milieu is to open the door to ways of becoming the master of it. We cannot control or change the wholly unknown. But when the components of a situation are known and understood, then, even though they may be unfair or undesirable, we know what we have to deal with and can plan and work accordingly.

The reason for the previous exposé lies in my belief that we can become most constructive when we understand the dynamics of our culture as they affect our particular situation and the dynamics of our personalities as they respond to cultural influences. I believe, therefore, that we should work at developing both broad and incisive understandings.

1) Understand your situation in historical perspective. I suggest that you keep alert to the status and role of single women throughout history. You are not likely to find books written on the topic or even very many direct references to the subject. You will find it in incidental references to, or portrayals of, single women in fiction or biographies or poetry of earlier periods. Having discovered what it has been, then try to discover why it has been that way. This will be more difficult, but if you raise enough questions and watch for the answers, you may get some clues. Here are a few questions with which to start your search:

Why have married persons scorned the unmarried, when so many of the former have been desperately unhappy?

Why have married women so often feared and resented single women?

What is it that causes married persons to pity single women?

What have single women done to provoke adverse attitudes from the general society?

Compare, then, the present attitude of our culture to that of the past. Try to see what changes are coming about and why. In brief, know something of what has been, what presently is, and what likely will be the status and role of the single woman in America. Then narrow this down to the particular geographical area, vocational activity, and religious affiliation which typify your situation. When you have done this, you should have a fairly clear general picture of things as they are for you.

Understand yourself. This is terribly important! That is why I ran the risk of pulling out all those ugly devices and attitudes that lurk about in the dark corners of an individual waiting to overtake her when she does not understand herself and these feelings.

Understanding yourself calls for relentless honesty. You need to face yourself frankly to see if any of these deviant attitudes and devices exist in you and then try to understand why you feel and react as you do. Unless you are honest you will employ a host of alibis, defenses, and rationalizations which will make it impossible for you to deal with yourself in your situation.

If you can find another single woman who will covenant with you to strive for honesty in the effort to understand your personal and spiritual problems, this type of open sharing can be most helpful. By the same token a shared relationship of defenses, alibis, and rationalizations can be very hurtful.

Understand others. I am thinking first of all of those others not in the single women's circle. Especially the others who are negative in their attitudes toward you. This will call for a look at yourselves as well as at the others. How responsible are you for the negative feelings of persons to whom you relate? Why do they feel about you as they do? Have you stimulated their adverse attitudes? If so, how have you done it and what can you now do about it?

If you are convinced that you are not responsible, then you need to try to understand why they need to ridicule or downgrade others. Are they projecting their own insecurities or feelings of inadequacy upon you as scapegoats because they feel our culture has given them license to do so? Do they somehow feel that you are a threat to them? Do some of them actually envy you and therefore try to hurt you? Understanding these others may not fully eliminate the relationship problems, but it can remove some of the personal sting and help you to be more tolerant of the persons involved.

Intolerance within the circle of the unmarried is frequently very strong also. It seems that they find it very difficult to tolerate in others the problems they find in themselves. The same genuine effort to understand is imperative in these relationships.

## *Take an objective look at life.*

There are some facts of life that must be recognized and taken into consideration if we are to have anything nearly like an unbiased view of life. Please look at a sampling of these with me.

Everybody has problems. I mentioned previously that tall girls have one set of problems. Left-handed people have another set. Teenagers have problems of their own. Senior citizens have a special packet of problems. Married people have a category of problems. And single women have problems, too.

It would be ridiculous to claim either that we do not have problems peculiar to our own group status or that we have all the problems and some other group has none. But problems do not necessarily mean that life is not worth living or even that it is a very troublesome existence. Problems may be stepping-stones to enlarged vision and broad understandings as you work through and resolve them.

So don't let the problems of the single woman get you down. Perk up and work at them! And remember that this is just what everybody else, yes, everybody else, has to do.

Marriage is not the answer to all problems. The flood of literature aimed at helping married persons with their problems and the record of the divorce courts should disillusion any single woman who thinks that marching to the marriage altar is the automatic solution to all of her problems. Women take many of their personal problems along with them into marriage and need to continue working at them there. It is certainly true that a good marriage will modify or erase many problems, but then it is also true that the changes and adjustments required by marriage may give rise to a new set of problems.

If you are a normal woman you are almost certain to desire marriage. God has created us male and female and has instituted marriage and family. While He has not decreed that all shall marry nor even made that possible, He has placed within both man and woman the desire to share life with a member of the opposite sex.

So for you to be interested in men and to desire marriage is not something to deny or to be ashamed of. I am tempted to become quite impatient with married people who ridicule a single woman with such statements as, "She just wants a man!" or "All she needs is a husband!"

Certainly you will not want to stimulate this desire if marriage is not in prospect for you, but neither do you want to deny or crush it. Rather, thank God for this evidence that you are a womanly woman with normal interests, even though the lack of fulfillment may at times bring suffering.

There are not available, suitable men for all women. We looked at the general surplus of women and the specific accentuation of this situation in certain geographical and professional areas. So now I'm saying, let's face the facts. Many women must remain unmarried in our monogamous society. Is there a reason why you should not be among them?

Not all men choose wisely. I referred earlier to the tendency among us to wonder what is the matter with a woman who does not marry. There seems to be an unwholesome compulsion to find fault in the single woman upon which to place the blame for her singleness. People seldom recognize that a particular woman's singleness may just as often be due to a man's faulty choosing as it is to the woman's undesirability. Often a man is captivated by a pretty face, a lovely figure, or a charming manner only to discover too late that these alone are not enough to make a good marriage. The doting husband soon discovers that the qualities which really count in marriage and home building are seriously lacking in the woman he married.

The fact that a woman has married is not saying that she has the qualities that make her suitable for marriage. By the same token, the fact that a woman is unmarried is no proof whatsoever that she lacks qualities of strength and suitability for marriage. Either case may simply be evidence of some man's pitiful lack of wisdom and his failure to choose well.

Rebellion intensifies problems. There is a sense in which each woman must identify and accept her own problems before she is in a position to deal with them creatively. This is true of many types of problems. If you consider being single a problem and you are rebellious about it and cannot tolerate yourself as a single person, or to say it another way, if you cannot accept singleness as a likely permanent status for yourself or others, you are almost certain to develop a fair share of the personality problems referred to earlier.

Marriage is not in God's plan for all women. The numerical inequality of men and women is clear evidence of this. Then there are certain physical and emotional handicaps that prohibit marriage. And there are some tasks to which women feel called of God that simply cancel out the possibility of marriage and family and homemaking as we know it.

I have watched some of the women of this latter group carrying heavy institutional responsibilities. I have seen others serving in hazardous situations in foreign countries. I have known them moving about from place to place in primitive lands with a freedom that only a lone individual, free to move according to need and expediency, could know. I have observed and listened to their sense of being called of the Lord and of being in His will.

And then I have remembered the words of a mission statesman who has traveled around the globe many times visiting church and mission points in many lands. He said, "You know, many times as I have observed single women at work in key positions in the church around the world, I have felt very keenly that God has kept many of the church's finest women single because He had special tasks for them to do that they could not have accomplished as married women with families." A review of the history of missions and of the church in the past century will yield abundant evidence of this observation.

Our culture holds superior opportunities for single women. We have said much about our society's adverse evaluation of women's singleness and the problems this precipitates. In all fairness, we must also say that conditions for the single woman really have improved over what they were fifty or seventy-five years ago.

The older folks among us still remember many of the single women they knew in their communities or families as the women who lived at home with their parents and took care of them during their declining years, or else they lived in the home of a married brother or sister and depended on them for security while in turn they helped them rear their families. If neither of these plans were possibilities, they moved about the community from home to home as they were needed, taking care of the sick, helping mothers with new babies, cleaning house in the spring and fall, or stepping into other strategic situations as they arose. Their wages were often very low, their work was usually the hard work of the community, and their live-in situations often meant that they had little time or privacy of their own. While many of them were loved and treated as friends by the families they served, there was also the tendency in many instances to take them and their services for granted; it was just their obligation to help out if anyone needed them. Little thought was given to them as persons of worth who might have wishes or rights of their own. Their role in the church was commonly one of inactivity. There were, of course, exceptions to this very general picture.

But in my own lifetime there has come about a great change and many times throughout my younger days I heard distraught mothers lament the passing of the good old days when you could find a hired woman to come into the home in emergencies to take over the hard work for a few dollars a week.

As people became more mobile, single women began to find their way into the cities where they could locate lighter work with higher wages and with more free time to develop interests of their own. As the level of required education advanced, many young women went into the professions and were able to live with a previously unknown independence. With the continued move into higher education an almost unbelievable selection of opportunities has developed for them.

As a result of all this change, many of you today are able to establish yourselves independently in your own homes where you are privileged to cultivate and express your interests. In many ways you may live very much like your married sisters.

With the development of Christian education and missions, Sunday schools, Bible schools, mission posts at home and abroad, summer camps, institutions of health and of general education, there has come a new day of activity and service opportunity for you in the life of the church.

It is also true that our culture and society hold superior opportunities for single women as compared with many other areas of the world.

Several years ago our next door international student neighbors from East Africa spoke frankly of their amazement that single women in America, such as my sister and I, could have homes and automobiles of their own and could pursue vocational interests that resulted in a good income and be respected individuals in the community and church. "In our country," they said, "there is no place, there is nothing, for an unmarried woman."

Several years later I stood among the crowd of people milling around outside of one of the churches near Uyo, East Nigeria, talking with a well-known Nigerian church leader. He wondered about my children. I told him that I was my husband's second wife, that I had married in later middle age, and that I had no children by birth. I continued to explain to him something of God's call to me in my younger years to serve Him in a role which I could not have fulfilled if I had raised a family of children. When I finished, he responded with a mixture of wonder and admiration. "You know," he said, "in your country it is so different! Here it is a very deep disgrace if a woman does not give birth to children. But you can live a happy, useful life; you do not need to feel disgraced if you are not a wife and mother. This is something very different and very wonderful."

Briefly then, with all the disadvantages we know here and now, we had better face it that comparatively speaking single women have it mighty good.

There are advantages in the single life. Never doubt it, there have been many unhappily married women who looked with thinly veiled envy at some of their single sisters and the rights and privileges of their singlehood!

There are certain advantages to being single that are significant in varying degrees depending upon the personality needs and interests of the persons considering them.

Independence is one of these advantages. Most of us have conflicting dependence-independence needs. Usually one or the other is in the ascendance most of the time. If our need for independence is quite strong, then the opportunities that the single life affords to plan one's own life, to make one's own decisions, to earn and spend one's own money, and to go and come at will may be a highly prized advantage.

Career privileges may be a real advantage for some single women. While it is true that many married women are career women too, it is also true that many married women are cut off from pursuing careers that they are deeply interested in. Usually the single woman can turn her time and interest into her profession or career with little distraction. She can come nearer knowing the satisfaction of undivided interest in a significant role or project.

Not all women enjoy preparing food and

running a household and rearing children. The thought of this kind of involvement is very burdensome to them. To such women the near-freedom from domestic responsibility which singlehood permits is a decided advantage.

Then there are some women for whom mobility holds a top priority. The romance of travel and the right to change living arrangements and employment at will are highly prized. Singleness makes it much more possible for them to keep on the move.

And many single women have opportunities for personal development and life enrichment that are denied many busy mothers involved in providing for the needs of their children.

### *Become the sort of women that are a credit to singleness.*

I was in my late teens, dating sporadically, but beginning to wonder whether I would marry. Perhaps I would remain single most or all of my life. In those days the Lord led me frequently to cross paths with one of His choice children, Miss Kathryn R. She was a registered nurse and the superintendent of a rather elite Main Line convalescent home for men. Intelligent, warm natured, capable, poised, gracious, feminine, and deeply spiritual, Miss R. had ministered to the lives of many, many people. One learned in myriad ways that through her, new meaning in life had come to many persons.

I observed her, listened to her, shared with her, and listened to what others said about her. There finally came a time when I vowed that if I remained single I would try in my own way to be as fine and admirable an edition of single womanhood as Miss R. The challenge to be the loveliest single woman ever, was rather intriguing to me as I saw the credit that this woman was to singlehood.

How can a woman today become a credit to the single life?

Develop positive attitudes. We've talked about a whole seedbed of negative attitudes that tend to sprout and grow in the personalities of single women as a result of adverse elements in their surroundings. We saw how these destructive forces militate against a woman's personal well-being and her effectiveness in interpersonal relationships. Now let's try to discover the cluster of positive attitudes that will resolve the negative factors and build constructive elements in a woman's life and relationships.

In the first place, remember that you are a person of worth. As a being created by God in His image you are of inestimable worth. No other of His created beings is of greater worth and no other human being is in a position to question your worth as a person. God esteems you, His workmanship, of so great worth that He loves you supremely and gave His Son to die so that you might live eternally. How foolish it is of any human being to try to depreciate the worth of another human being so loved by God!

This fact of worth is not cause for personal pride, but it is reason for deep gratitude and a response of dignity. As God's created being you have as much right to walk with head erect as any other person. And marriage or singleness does not add to or detract from your worth and from this right one little bit. Please don't forget it — even when other people try subtly to convince you otherwise.

Remember also that you are a woman, a real woman, and that neither marriage nor singleness necessarily changes the quality of your womanliness. True, it will determine to some extent the avenues of expressing your womanly characteristics, but you are first of all a woman with all that means and only secondarily a married or single woman.

Positive attitudes will also include acceptance of your singleness. I am not referring to an acceptance so final that you close the door to every possibility of marriage. Even though you have a quiet assurance that God has led you into your present status, you will still need to recognize that He has the right to lead you out of it. But the problem is not usually one of final acceptance of singleness but one of accepting it at all.

Until you can get beyond thinking of your

singleness as merely an interim stage before marriage you are in no position to live life fully and thus become a woman at her best. When a woman can accept singleness as her particular status, then she can begin to explore its possibilities for life fulfillment; she can live vibrantly in the now of her life.

Another important phase of acceptance is the acceptance of mounting age. Be the age you are and glorify that age rather than trying to deceive people into believing that you are much younger than you really are. You know, they usually learn your actual age anyhow and then they are likely to judge you as immature rather than clever. Why does a Christian woman want to be deceitful anyhow?

A single person needs to care about her personal development. There is a tendency among many single persons to find security in sameness or routine or being in a "groove." But if this is not guarded carefully, it can mean the fossilizing of the person. So while there must be enough little rituals in a woman's life to keep her comfortable, there must be many types of personal development going on at the same time.

When have you last wrestled with great ideas that stretched your mind, took you out of your little world and away beyond yourself? Have you wrestled with ideas of religious philosophy, of technology, of psychology, or of social thought? At least occasionally you should subject yourself to books or lectures or seminars that expand your horizons in areas that are not related to your areas of special interest.

When have you last expanded your social experiences? Have you been doing the same things with the same little circle of friends for a long time? Or have you discovered new types of social experiences through the years?

What about your skills and creative interests? Do you have a very limited list of things that you can do and find satisfaction in doing them? Or are you constantly adding to this list and strengthening the interests you already have?

What has been happening to you spiritually in the past five years? Are you on very much the same plane that you were then? Or have you regressed so that you cannot even say with confidence that your spiritual life is as significant to you now as it was then? Hopefully neither of these possibilities describes you, but rather, you are developing and maturing and making profound discoveries in your walk with the Lord. To develop intellectually, socially, creatively, and spiritually is to move toward becoming the kind of woman that is a credit to singlehood.

6) It is also important to be a self-giving person. Becoming the sort of woman that is a credit to your status is not all a matter of receiving or retaining within yourself certain

qualities. The law of giving in order to become is especially significant to the lone individual; in one respect it is the law of life for her. I think I am correct in saying that the tendency to become selfish or to express selfishness is intensified for single women for two reasons.

In the first place, the demands for self-giving (1) that are inherent in living with a husband and children are missing. One does not have occasions around her at every turn in her home to think of the wishes, rights, and pleasures of other persons and so she just naturally thinks of her own pleasure and desires.

In the second place, because you do not have (2) these natural avenues of self-giving and thoughtful interest in another's good you find it much more difficult to take initiative and discover ways of reaching out and contributing to persons around you. If you happen to be a reserved, sensitive person, you are always aware that what you have to offer may not be acceptable to the other person and so, rather than run the risk of being rejected or hurt otherwise, you turn your interests back on yourself. This means a slow but certain death to positive personality development.

If you can accept the fact that there may be occasional rebuffs and rejections of your efforts to be self-giving, but go ahead anyhow to share what you are, even more than what you have, you will find yourself bringing life to others as well as to yourself.

If you need stimulating ideas on how to be self-giving, I suggest you find a copy of David Dunn's *Try Giving Yourself Away*[2] and then use your own creative powers and ideas for sharing yourself.

7) You can also be the sort of women that are a credit to the single status by their personal discipline of moral integrity.

I have mentioned previously some of the moral testings that arise from social, psychological, and biological needs and drives. When all of these converge to strengthen certain drives, the single woman may have on hand a fierce battle that calls for strong inner resources and perhaps even for help from outside of herself. If this were not the case, the increasing number of moral casualties in our society, including those within the church, would hardly exist.

What does a woman do with her desires for intimate male companionship? What does she do with her longing for children of her own? What does she do with the buildup of sexual tension which may be the result either of her normal biological cycle or of sex stimuli that abound in her environment? There are no easy answers and I would be unfair if I were to pretend that there are.

Some women decide it is not worth the fight

2. David Dunn, *Try Giving Yourself Away* (Scarsdale, N.Y.: The Updegraff Press, Ltd., 1947).

and in one way or another they yield to deviant behavior either in illicit relationships with a member of either sex or in solitary personal sexual exploitation. They say they just can't help it. Eventually any one of these types of expressions leads to loss of self-respect, to feelings of defeat and of guilt, and each of these contributes to personality deterioration and spiritual conflict.

Some women retain the form of morality, but within themselves they are frequently guilty of immoral fantasies. They feed their minds with literature and films and conversations that contribute to sexual stimulation and develop a morbid curiosity about sex.

Some women become angry with God and blame Him for giving them needs and drives that have to be restrained. They blame Him for cutting them off from legitimate fulfillment.

Is there then no way for a woman to retain her moral integrity and personality integration in a sex-oriented culture such as ours with internal and external forces rallied for her defeat?

Let me share a few ideas and suggestions that may have significance for you.

Use your head. Think through this complex problem at a time when the blood runs cool in your veins and you can look at the matter with an objective perspective.

Remember, for instance, that there are millions upon millions of people in the world with unmet needs and hungers, persons who are hungry for food, or lacking in physical security, or health, or fellowship, or love of any sort. Each one has just as much right as you have to blame God for giving him desires and needs which must frequently or regularly remain unfulfilled. Most of them keep on living and so can you. The possibility of life having meaning and significance for us does not depend on having all of life's hungers fulfilled all of the time.

Did you ever hear of "no-salt" diet or "sugar-free" diet? To partake of the forbidden substance has fatal consequences. That does not take the desire away, but people do without anyway. The tension exists, but the dieter refrains and lives. I'll let you make the application.

Discipline yourself to avoid situations and activities that you find sexually stimulating. (These will not be the same for all women.) Generally, literature, films, music, and conversation with undue emphasis on sex are questionable diet for anyone and are often especially frustrating for single persons.

Discipline yourself to change activities when you discover that you are being stimulated to the point of frustration. If reading that book while you are comfortably snuggled among your pillows and blankets stimulates you fiercely, get out of your nest, lay your book aside at least temporarily if not permanently, get a drink of ice water, play a lively tune on the piano, and read a children's story and likely you will find the storm has gone and calm is restored.

Commit the sexual part of your being to the keeping power of God in the dedication of your total self to Him.

We have other areas of temptation and testing that plague us in our mortal bodies. We bring these to God and claim His strength to live above them. In the same way we need to deal with the temptations arising from the sexual aspect of our beings.

While sex drives and desires are good in themselves and are not sinful, they are avenues to sin for persons who respond to them illicitly. They must therefore be kept in reserve and under control. The Christian woman finds her will strengthened and her way kept in this area as in others as she gives herself to God in dedication to His purpose for her life.

I would like to underscore the fact that there is a real difference between temptation and sin in the area of sex just as certainly as this is true in any other area of life. For a woman to experience deep sexual desire and be aware of the possible ways of responding to her drives need not be sin. Many women are confused and suffer a needless sense of guilt because they think each surge of desire for an intimate relationship and each recognition of potential for intimate sharing with another person is sin. Sin does not lie in the possession of a sexual nature nor in the recognition of the sexual attractiveness of another person. It lies rather in the stimulating and feeding of sexual desire, the reveling in covetous sexual fantasy, and in the overt illicit expressions of the sexual phase of a woman's being.

Remember the grace and forgiveness of God.

There are likely some of you who are thinking: "Yes, it's all very well to talk about how to deal with your drives and keep yourself out of trouble, but it's too late for me. I didn't have help when I needed it and now I have to live with this blot on me for the rest of my life. Even though other people don't know about it, I do, and it plagues me endlessly!"

It is true that our wrongs can never be undone. This is just as true of any other sin as it is of a sex transgression. But it is also true that the grace and forgiveness of God are just as abundant for the person whose sin is sexual as it is for the person who has committed any other sin — and we have all sinned. He means for you to face life with humility and with confidence in His work of renewing and keeping. (For many women the cleansing, renewing work of the Lord seems to be realized more clearly when the confession and commitment take place in the presence of a respected Christian counselor.)

You may also be a credit to the single status

by being real women. What a dangerous, elastic term to use — real women! That could mean different things to different people. Let me say it this way: You may be a credit to the single status by giving full expression to the common characteristics of womanhood which can be appropriately expressed by Christian single women.

What are some of these characteristics?

In an age when woman and her role are considered from such divergent views, we gain our sense of understanding of God's view of her by looking into His Word.

We discover in the first place that God created her to bring completeness to the human race. Wonderful creature though Adam was, he was lacking in certain qualities. God gave woman to fill or make up for these lacks and needs and thus to bring completeness.

We can say then that real women are here to be a complement to men. I can hear some of you say, "Why tell us what we already know but dare not experience?" My answer is that, while in its most intimate expression this refers to marriage, in its broader expression this refers to general social relationships.

Unfortunately far too many women get the idea that since they are not married, they must live in competition with men. While there may be an element of truth in this as it applies to the world of work, I hold that even here there are many opportunities for complementing the male personality and qualities. Woman's greatest service and fulfillment is not in becoming like a man to compete with men, but rather in enriching and expressing her womanly qualities in order to be a complement to man.

From the very first record we have of the relationship of man and woman we recognize that woman holds a tremendous influence over man. This has not decreased through the centuries. With the passing of time I am becoming more and more convinced of the strength of this influence. Mother Eve and untold numbers of women who have followed her have misused this power. Women of God use it, often unknowingly, for Him and for good. Again, this power of influence is not limited to the marriage relationship, to a wife's influence on her husband. It has its broader expressions wherever men and women are related to each other in social and service activities.

Considering woman's influence, James Stalker writes, "The influence of women is subtle and remote; but it is on this account all the more powerful; for they sit at the very fountains, where the river of human life is springing, and where a touch may determine its entire subsequent course."[3]

Stalker's statement reminds us by its veiled

3. James Stalker, *The Trial and Death of Jesus Christ* (Grand Rapids, Mich.: Zondervan Publishing House), p. 91.

reference that real women are bearers and nurturers of life. God has called women to this breathtaking role of being co-creators and sustainers of life with Him. Again you may say that you are cut off from the right to bring a human being to life by giving birth. And again you are correct. But you are not deprived of the right to nurture and enrich life.

It seems to me that it is no chance occurrence that most of the nurses in our country are women — right there by the bedside fighting for life, nurturing and affirming it. Nor is it by chance that most teachers of small children are women. They are right there filling the role of nurture. These roles and similar or related ones are wide open for single women to give expression, under God, to many qualities of womanhood.

This idea of real women being co-creators and co-nourishers with God, of life, is not limited to involvement in physical finite life. It finds its greatest expression in the spiritual life. In this there is no limitation placed by marriage status. In fact, singleness seems to be an advantage, for Paul says, "The unmarried woman careth for the things of the Lord . . ." (1 Corinthians 7:34). Entering into intimate spiritual relationship with God, she brings people to spiritual birth and spends years in nurturing them. The delight and satisfaction she experiences from knowing that an eternal life has begun and is growing in a mortal being is transcendent!

Real women express many of the finest qualities of life and personality. The apostles Paul and Peter were sensitive to the elements of spirit and personality that revealed womanhood at its highest.[4] They were also quick to recognize perversions of womanliness. From them we learn that real women are beautiful in the "inmost center" of their beings. We learn that they are characterized by such spiritual qualities as faith, love, purity, reverence, and humility. These then find expression in gentleness of manner and conduct, in quietness of heart and demeanor, in modesty of appearance and behavior, in submission of self in human relationships, and in good deeds to all people.

What a contrast to the western world's twentieth-century ideal of woman! But it is God's portrayal of genuine womanhood. And the challenge to be this kind of woman is not limited by singleness!

If you are to become the sort of woman that is a credit to singleness, you will need to develop spiritually. The personality of Jesus should be developing in your life. It is beautiful wherever it is expressed and is not hindered by the unmarried state.

Devotion to Christ and His will has in it the antidote or the answer to all of the undesirable

4. 1 Timothy 2:9-15; 1 Peter 3:1-6.

attitudes with their resulting personality problems which we looked at earlier. I know that is a tremendous and daring statement, but I believe it is true. Let me hasten to say, however, that God gives a lifetime in which to learn to apply truth to the business of living. So if you have not yet found Christ's answer to some of your needs, consider it an adventure to continue in the process of discovering and appropriating what meanings He has for your life.

# 6

## The Best That Life Offers

Many single women feel that they have been cheated out of God's best for them by missing marriage and motherhood. It is no wonder that they feel this way if they have listened to the prevailing attitudes of society and the church. It is highly important that you take your New Testament and try to discover what it says about this matter.

The fact that Jesus Himself found it possible and preferable to live and do His work for the salvation of humanity as a single person is significant. Marriage was not a requirement for perfection of personhood or fulfillment of the highest purposes in His life. It is the privilege of the single adult to identify with Him in His singleness.

Furthermore, His favorite place of fellowship and relaxation was in the home of three persons who apparently were single; the home of Mary, Martha, and Lazarus. He loved these people and shared deeply in their lives. Perhaps their very singleness made them more receptive to Him.

At all times Jesus was respectful of marriage and family life as an important institution for earth living, but His primary emphasis was on building the kingdom of God. The former was subservient to the latter. He made it very clear that family ties and loyalties must be secondary for His followers.

The Apostle Paul, who also appears to have been a single man, promotes this same attitude. Some of the most sublime passages in the New Testament regarding marriage and family relationships were written by Paul. And yet he, too, sees the God-man relationship, and what marriage or singleness contributes to kingdom building as of transcendent importance.

Dr. M. D. Hugen points out that "The coming of Christ has relativized the significance of marriage and parenthood."[5] He implies that the togetherness of the church has in part replaced the sharing, the participating, and the partnership of the family.

Read the New Testament with open minds on this matter and you will see there are very

5. Hugen, *op. cit.*, p. 48.

few records on marital status. Little is said about the Lord's followers as to who was married to whom, or whether or not they were married at all. We read very little about the families of the saints. What we do find is how one saint ministered to the needs of another, how the saints loved each other, and how they shared in the fellowship and work of the church of Jesus Christ.

Clearly, in the mind of God, the most important thing about a women is not whether she is single or married, but whether she is rightly related to the Lord and His church. Whether she is single or married is important only as this relates to the will of God for her life.

When it really begins to dawn on you that singleness does not limit you in your reach for the highest achievements whether in time or eternity, you become able to open yourself more freely to know the fullness of Christ in your life as a single person.

Christian single women often ask: "Can Christ really satisfy the unmarried woman?" or "How can a single woman find complete satisfaction in Christ?" From close sharing with unmarried women I have concluded that these questions in their broad implications haunt and perplex many women.

If you happen to be a younger woman who is still dating now and then, you probably look at women who are beyond the usual dating age and wonder if Christ satisfies and meets their needs. If you have already left the dating crowds and are trying to adjust to a way of life for which you have had no positive orientation, you may be wrestling with various conflicts and questionings: "But isn't it possible for Jesus to satisfy my longings? Isn't there something wrong with my relationship to the Lord if Jesus doesn't satisfy me and I'm discontent and full of longing?"

This is not a simple matter through which to find one's way, but it must be faced realistically before we are in a position to talk very knowingly about cultivating our spiritual resources. This one question, "Can Christ really satisfy the unmarried woman?" raises a host of other questions that can be approached knowingly only as we recall the cultural, social, and biological factors influencing the single woman's life.

Remember that in our culture the single woman encounters terrific social pressures. They tend to intensify dissatisfactions which she may have. The western world, including the Protestant community in its swing away from the celibacy of Catholicism, has glorified marriage. It regards marriage as the one honorable state for woman and ridicules and stereotypes the unmarried woman continually. The American culture is emphasizing sex in an almost primitively pagan manner so that it is kept before the minds of the people more than any one other single idea.

Remember too that in social activities our culture revolves around couples. Many times a single woman feels almost forced to accept the company of a man in whom she has no personal interest in order to conform socially and fit into the social situation.

Then remember also that for many people the drives toward intimate sharing spiritually, intellectually, and physically are among some of the stronger if not the strongest drives which they possess. When these are continually bombarded by the cultural and social emphases, they are stimulated and overdeveloped until the single woman finds herself with desires and needs that are exaggerated far beyond their true importance.

In the face of all this many Christian women despair and say, "Can Christ really satisfy these?"

Now let me ask you a few questions about this major question which we have been repeating in various forms. What do you mean by this question? Do you mean, "Does having Christ in your life take away your desire to be married, or keep you from missing the companionship of a husband, or erase your biological hungers for sex fulfillment?" Is this what you mean when you say, "Can Christ really satisfy the unmarried woman?"

If this is what you mean, are you implying then that Christian women who do marry have not found Christ satisfying and have married because He did not satisfy? If this is the case, is it not just as logical to ask, Can Christ really satisfy the married woman? What or who does satisfy her, her husband or Christ?

What inner needs do we have a right to ask Christ to satisfy? We have many needs and drives: hunger, thirst, sex, the need for rest, companionship, love, achievement, and so on. Does having Christ in our lives cancel these needs and drives? No, we keep on getting hungry and thirsty and needing rest and human companionship, don't we? A woman becomes a Christian, but her basic needs and drives remain the same. A happily married woman may be very mature in her Christian experience, but if her husband dies and their relationship has been a satisfying one, she is going to have some unmet drives and hungers. No one, Christians included, expects it to be otherwise. Why should we expect it to be otherwise for any woman without a husband? Women are made up much alike, you know.

Can a woman then, conscious of unmet needs and drives in her life, really say that Jesus meets the deepest longings and needs of the soul? The answer is "yes." She can say it, for He does it. But what are the soul's deepest needs? There are deeper needs than the need for social approval, for material security, for sex fulfillment, or all the rest of the generally recognized human needs. Deeper than these are the spiritual needs:

Our need for forgiveness.
Our need for freedom from guilt.
Our need for assurance of salvation.
Our need of hope for time and eternity.
Our need for a sense of meaning in life.
Our need for purpose in the scheme of things.
Our need for motivation with eternal meanings.
Our need for fellowship with the Divine.

Many a woman may have in full measure such things as social approval, sex fulfillment, and financial security and be lacking forgiveness, salvation, purpose, and all of the other spiritual needs and thus be in deep poverty. On the other hand, many women who have experienced the latter apart from the former have been comparatively rich and satisfied.

You may be saying, "Yes, if one has to choose between the spiritual satisfactions and the temporal, short-lived satisfactions, I'll choose the spiritual." But I hear some of you add, "A lot of people don't need to choose; they have both!"

This is true. But may I remind you again that the large majority of Christians in the world live with unmet needs of one sort or another. For some reason God chooses to permit many Christians to have their need for food unmet. And many others have their need for physical security unfulfilled. It is more typical than atypical for us to live with some unmet needs and hungers.

Now I suspect some of you are thinking: Then you mean to say that Christ doesn't really have anything to offer to the single woman's loneliness, lack of companionship, lack of security in love, deep biological hungers, and the like; these are just simply the unmet needs she has to live with and that is that!

No, I am not saying that, because I know by my own experience and from the testimony of others that having Christ does make a difference. Having Him in our lives does not eradicate the drives, hungers, and needs with which He created us but it does put them in their proper place in relation to the realities of time and eternity and this can make a great difference for us since so often our needs for this life have become so exaggerated. Let me explain how this makes a difference.

I am convinced that the terrific drive for status, the extreme interest in food, and the obsession with sex which characterize the American culture today are striking indications of empty, meaningless lives. I am just as certain that when a person becomes vibrantly alive to Christ these things take a different place. For instance, a Christian woman is grateful when others think well of her, but her primary concern is the approval of Jesus Christ, and the awful compulsion to seek status among people is minimized. She continues to be grateful for food and enjoys it, but she no longer lives to eat but eats to live because she has more important things to do with her life. And if certain of her needs are not fully met, she is not crushed because of the lack, for her very deepest needs are taken care of.

What I'm trying to point up is that when Christ has His proper place in our lives, other things take their proper place, which is a subordinate place. The more completely Christ has the preeminence in our lives, the more our time, interest, affections, and goals are wrapped up in Him and the less we are obsessed with things that are temporal or passing; not that they will necessarily hold no interest for us but they will not possess and control us.

You may call this sublimation if you will; this is a good word and an experience that is common to us all. The diabetic person may love sweets and decide to have them at any cost and die as a result, or she may refuse to cater to that hunger, develop other legitimate tastes, and live well in spite of being denied sugar.

The unmarried woman may have strong drives for male companionship and have it at any cost to her ruination, or she may turn away from what is not rightfully hers and find in her spiritual pursuits that which enriches her life to the extent that she has little time or desire to mourn that of which she has been deprived.

How does one become involved with Christ so that He becomes primary in our lives and the man-woman relationship with its related needs becomes secondary?

Many women find singleness a stumbling block to a relaxed faith in God and so they are cut off from realizing many of the satisfactions that come to the person who does believe in His personal interest in her life. They cannot quite believe that God is actively involved in their lives. Or if they believe He is involved, they are unable to accept as good the situation they are in. It is highly important that we have confidence in God and are assured of His involvement in our lives for our good, all other propaganda notwithstanding.

If we could see with the omniscience of God all the factors unknown to us which affect and enter into the shaping of our lives, we would have no question of His love and goodness. But we are finitely limited in this and so we turn to His Word and bathe our hearts again and again in the great fact that He loved us so much that He gave us His Son. And we rest again in the assurance that such love can be trusted with the details of our lives. In this confidence we open up our hearts to the active involvement of Christ in our lives. We are ready to enter into a satisfying, creative relationship with Him.

How then do we nurture and strengthen and develop this relationship until it has the preeminence among our relationships? How do we nurture and strengthen and develop any relationships involving two persons? How would you proceed to build a strong, creative relationship with another person whom you felt to be eminently superior to yourself in every way? Your answers to these questions may be your clues to a strengthened relationship with the Lord Jesus. You need to learn to know the Lord by all the means that are open to you. And they are many.

Through His Word you may become deeply and intimately acquainted with His thoughts and ways and will. I cannot overemphasize the importance of studying the Word and meditating upon its message. Read until your mind and heart are saturated with it and it becomes merged inextricably into your character. Meditate until your vision of the Lord enlarges and becomes so clear and marvelous that you find yourself joining with the multitudes in the Revelation saying, "Worthy is the Lamb that was slain to receive power, and riches, and wisdom, and strength, and honour, and glory, and blessing" (Revelation 5:12). Both a careful, systematic study of the Word and a relaxed, devotional approach to it are recommended for your quest to know Him.

We learn to know Him, too, through prayer, through conversing with Him. To a great extent the study of the Word and prayer become two phases of one experience, the conversation of a person and her Lord. God speaks to you as you read and you respond at that moment with praise or confession or thanks or a question or a commitment. In this way you find the Lord giving direction to your praying as He leads in the conversation, and your delight in such an intimate fellowship enlarges.

The Holy Spirit reveals the Lord Jesus to us also as we open ourselves to be taught of Him. Through Him the Lord Jesus becomes the comforter who stands with us to "help us cope with things as they are."

We learn to know the Lord as this preeminent One through the church. Earlier I said a number of things about the church's attitudes toward the single woman that were not very complimentary. I cannot deny these now, for I believe they are true. But it is also true that all institutions made up of human beings are imperfect and need always to be growing in understanding. Even though the church is made up of redeemed people, they are still human beings with this same need of developing understanding. We cannot cancel out the fine aspects of the church and cut ourselves off from its blessings just because some of its members have a blind spot that allows them to have adverse attitudes toward single women. Furthermore we must recognize that there is a growing understanding among many church leaders of single adults and their problems and needs. Not a few groups of lay members are becoming aware of this, too.

The church is the body of Christ, the people of God, the custodian of the gospel. In her midst there is much that reveals Christ and that contributes to the development of the spiritual resources so important to the single woman, even though no effort may be made to relate truth to her specific needs.

We learn to know the Lord and His fullness in close spiritual fellowship with others. A woman needs a small group sharing experience where persons can be themselves in honest opening up of hearts and needs. There are settings where each can minister to the other of the Lord's grace in her life.

Our relationship to the Lord strengthens as we continue to affirm His position in our lives. We say yes to His word to us. We are warmly accepting of His will for us. We are responsive to His love to us. We are deeply grateful for His life in us. We are always affirming Him and becoming more and more of what He meant when He said, "I in them and they in me."

Our relationship to Him is clarified and strengthened as we introduce Him to others. Telling others what we know about Him has a way of enlarging our own vision of Him and increasing His preciousness to us. And the more we know Him and the more precious He becomes to us, the more we want to witness of Him.

Our relationship with the Lord continues to strengthen as we work with Him as partners in some Christian cause. We trust Him, we follow Him, we see what He accomplishes, and we are thrilled to be involved in undertakings that have eternal values.

A number of single women whom I have known personally for years come clearly into my thoughts. They are women who quite evidently have found the Lord Jesus and their relationship with Him a source of great satisfaction. This has made it possible for them to see life and their singleness in a proper perspective. I have known them as women of poise and serenity and yet of vibrancy. They are women of strength and courage and compassion, of depth and love and purpose. They are women who, having found Him and the blessings of His presence, have come to realize that nothing else matters quite so much in life as that others should find Him, too. And so they have given family, material possessions, and status all secondary or lower positions in their lives in order that their primary purpose of knowing Him and sharing Him may be realized.

The way they have taken and the blessing

they have found is open to each single woman who will give herself to the pursuit of Christ to be her life.

We've been talking about seeking and discovering the Lord and His will for our lives. When we've made these discoveries we have come into possession of the best that life has for us. But this abstract statement finds its actuality in many concrete ways. I would like to suggest a number of areas in which single women can search and find possibilities for experiencing and expressing the fullness of life of the person in touch with God.

I do not need to tell you that life without friends is hardly life at all. We have within us a deep need to share life in varying degrees with other persons. Our experiences of pleasure are intensified as we share them with others and our sufferings are lessened when a good friend gets under the load with us.

And yet many of us have scarcely begun to explore the possibilities of joy and mutual enrichment that friendship holds. We have several friends of "our kind" with whom we do almost everything. Living life through their eyes is almost the same as seeing it through ours. After a while we have very little to contribute to them nor do they to us except a measure of security in rescuing each other from stark aloneness. I suggest that the single woman make an effort to develop a wide friendship circle with a great diversity of types of persons within the circle.

There should be children of varying ages among your friends. You can be a favorite caller or "auntie" of a family of children and they can help you retain flexibility and a fresh outlook on life. (This relationship calls for sensitivity and tactfulness, especially in contacts with parents.) Generally you should keep your understanding of children to yourself unless it is asked for. Giving birth to a child does not necessarily create a good nurturing mother, I know. And if you are a carefully trained and experienced person in some area of child development, you may be way out ahead of the parents in understanding children, but this is an ouchy spot and being tactless about it is an almost certain way to invite derisive remarks such as, "Who does that old maid think she is! People that don't have kids of their own should keep quiet!"

There should be married persons among your friends, both married couples and married women. And if you are alive to life's possibilities for the single woman, you should have much to contribute to them. They too will be able to contribute wholesome influences to you. They are not so likely to be the people you go out with in our couple society. They are more comfortably the people you drop in to call on in their family setting or who very casually stop by to chat with you and share interest in your hobbies and in mutual church activities.

Again this calls for a fine sensitivity on your part so that the relationship with the husband does not become too familiar or the relationship with the wife does not become so possessive that it becomes a hindrance to their full sharing as husband and wife.

In this day of international mobility there should be persons of other cultures or races among your friends. Many of these persons in our country would be very grateful for someone to come close and acquaint them with life from the western point of view and share life with them. And while you share with them you too will have your horizons greatly widened.

Being friends with persons of other countries involves much more than giving them things. We know this with our minds, but we often act as though we are not aware of it. Sometimes our friends have the courage to tell us. A Japanese friend of mine once exclaimed with deep feeling, "You Americans! You know how to give us your things but you do not know how to give us yourselves!"

Senior citizens merit a place among our friends. They need us and we need them. We can help them stay in the mainstream of today and they can help us to round out our perspective of life. Recently I listened while a 93-year-old friend told with animation of his ministry among the churches of Virginia sixty years ago. What a revelation of a period that so significantly affected the present!

Among our friends there should be persons from differing social levels, from various ethnic groups, and from other vocational pursuits. An all-nurse or all-teacher friendship group can become very sterile. We need the stimulation of a broad variety of conversation content. The person with radically different circumstances or vocational interests can likely contribute very much in broadened awareness of life. And again it will be a reciprocal experience.

While you have this wide variety of friends with varying types of friendship you will always need that little core of "comfortable-as-an-old-shoe" friends. The kind that understand you and love you and accept you and share intimately with you. There is little need for me to even suggest that these should be among your friends — you know it instinctively and you count on them so fully that you face the dangerous temptation of letting them be sufficient for you. That would actually result in impoverishment of the other groups I've mentioned. So have them, but hold them lightly in your open hand; don't clutch them and destroy yourself and them.

Since I'm talking about these very close friends, I should remind you that occasionally one of these whom you thought you could depend on forever as an intimate standby is suddenly discovered by a man who also sees her potential as a delightful person with whom to share life. And almost before you can realize what is happening, she is about to be moved out of your cozy, secure little circle. Then what?

Some of you can take it very well. You had always kept this possibility in mind and kept prepared to make adjustments gracefully even though they might be painful.

But some of you are unprepared for the breaking up of your comfortable relationships and you find yourselves besieged by feelings and attitudes you can hardly understand and your reactions are something less than what you would have expected of yourself. You would hate to admit it, but deep down inside of yourself you resent the fact that this experience has come to your friend instead of you. You resent the person who is taking your friend's first affection and you resent having your comfort and security shaken or shattered.

Resentment is bound to be expressed and begins to crop out here and there. You begin to find fault with the way your friend carries on her new friendship. You criticize her marriage plans. You become venomous in your denunciation of the man she is to marry. You pick up every flaw, real or imagined, in his personality or character and magnify it many times over. You shake your head wisely, prophesy disaster for the couple, and declare how much better off you are in the single state. All this while persons not so emotionally involved are declaring this to be the logical "made-for-each-other" couple. Months later when you see your friend and her husband building a good life together, you still have to reckon with your resentments and the strained relationships you have brought about.

Finally, it is a common tendency of women to be very selective in their friendships. They reach for friends who will enhance their social standing or prestige. Or they seek out the persons they consider charming or those so like themselves that they feel very secure with them. I would like to challenge you to be looking for friends in unlikely situations among unlikely people. The discovery of value and worth in unexpected places can be one of the most exciting ventures in building friendships. I encourage you to think and act broadly and creatively about developing friendships. You will discover one of the best assets life has to offer.

What about the men among your friends? You notice I have not said specifically that there should be men among your friends. If there are respectable bachelors or widowed men in your acquaintance whose friendship is desirable and available, I rather suspect I need not be encouraging you to include them in your friendship circle.

However, in many areas of the country women above the mid-twenties find it almost impossible to hold a casual friendship with single men due to the pressure of society's attitudes as well as the personal involvement likely to develop on the part of one or the other person.

My nearest reference to your having men in your friendship circle was my reference to your having married couples among your friends. I specifically said married couples because I believe there is very little room for the developing and sharing of strong friendships between single women and married men that exclude the wife. Counselors and writers have indicated the great risks involved in this apparently innocent sort of relationship. Dr. Marion Hillyard speaking out of many years of observation and counseling in the medical profession says that as a doctor she does not believe there is "such a thing as a platonic relationship between a man and a women who are alone together a great deal." [6]

Keith Miller in *A Second Touch* included a chapter on "Responsible Loving Relationships Between Men and Women." [7] In this he recognizes that intimacy of spiritual sharing between men and women may make them especially vulnerable to social temptations. This possibility

6. Marion Hillyard, *A Woman Doctor Looks at Life and Love* (New York: Doubleday and Company, Inc., 1957), p. 91.
7. Keith Miller, *A Second Touch* (Waco, Texas: Word Books, 1967), p. 97.

is not a reflection on your character or the Christian experience of the married man. It is simply an honest recognition of male and female forces that exist in human beings, of the influence of spiritual, intellectual, and emotional compatibilities upon sexual responsiveness, and of the need for all of this to be safeguarded for the good of the individual and the larger institutions of home and church and for the honor of the Lord.

Stating it simply: Even though you are both Christians and think you can be sharing friends on a high spiritual level, you are putting yourself in a very dangerous position which is likely to end in suffering for one or both of you. You might as well face and accept the fact that the possibility of Christian single women having men as close friends is quite limited.

You should also consider your living arrangements. The place where you spend your time outside of your work hours has a significant effect on your well-being. Here is where you should be able to be yourself, to find a measure of security, to relax, to fellowship, and to recreate.

Shall this be a place of your own? In our culture few households are large enough for two generations of adults both of which have the capacity to manage themselves and their households. As long as your mother is able to manage her house she needs this right and responsibility. This means that if you live with her, you should keep your ideas and personality expressions in reserve. You cannot be the domestic head of the household even though you are years older than your married sister who is directing her household.

It is also apt to mean that many times you are not treated as the adult that you are and you therefore likely regress to, or retain, less mature behavior. Either you become withdrawn and inhibited in your home, or your mother becomes unduly dependent on you, or friction develops between you. (I am certain that there must be some exceptional cases in which adult mothers and daughters live together without harm to each other, but the arrangement seems to be predominantly an unsatisfactory one.)

So then, what do you do? If your work calls you into another community, the problem is not too difficult to solve. If you stay in your hometown, you may be tempted just to go rent a room in some other house. This may be a partial answer but hardly the best.

Many factors will enter into your decision regarding the type of housing you decide to make into your home. You may be limited in the area where you want to locate by what is available. You may be influenced as to the size of your home by your interest in entertaining. Your financial standing will likely be one of the main determiners. The stability of your employment will be significant also.

If you are financially able, you may decide to own or rent a small family-sized house. If maintenance and management of your own house is too big an undertaking for you, an apartment of several rooms may meet your need and stay within your means. Really the important thing is not so much that your home is large and elegant, but rather that it fits your needs and provides a place for you to express your interests and personality.

It should be a place that majors in convenience since single women usually need to learn to do housekeeping and entertaining in a minimum of time. It should provide genuine comfort for the hours you are privileged to spend in it. It should provide possibilities for some recreational activities and it should be appropriately arranged for entertaining.

Elegant, sedate, bohemian, rustic, formal, casual, or quaint — it should be the place where you feel at home because it is a sort of extension of you. For many years I have watched single women take anything from a square, boxlike room to a lovely full-sized house and let go with their imaginations to make a home that was truly a refuge.

Will you do it alone or will you find a housemate? Some of you will genuinely prefer to establish your home alone. Others will find aloneness unbearable. If you are one of the latter, there are a number of things to consider carefully before you settle on a housemate:

1. Not every good friend makes a good living companion. Maybe even your best friend "rubs you wrong" when you need to live in the same room or rooms. My closest woman friend of many years' standing and I had a commonly agreed upon understanding that the nearest we would try to live together would be in a duplex or adjoining apartments! Maybe you'd better at least spend a vacation together in the same cottage before you negotiate setting up housekeeping together.

2. Some similarity of taste in furnishings, common interests in recreation, agreement in views regarding finances, and the same level of income are all important.

3. Your housemate just may get married within a year or two after you've set up housekeeping and disrupt the whole arrangement!

On the other hand, if you are convinced that you have a compatible prospect and are willing to take the risk of possible disruption later on, it is quite possible that you may be able to develop an excellent living arrangement in which you will find companionship and shared responsibility for your home.

Such an arrangement is likely to be more satisfying if you and your friend choose the home and the furnishings together rather than one of you obtaining and furnishing the house and then inviting the other to come live with you.

Choosing wisely in the area of recreation and self-expression is important too. Married women are often driven by circumstances into the avocational activities related to homemaking. They tend to be somewhat limited in the choice of activities by the imminent needs of homemaking. But you are more likely to be able to survey the field and choose your recreational and expressional activities without a sense of necessity to concentrate in a particular area. This makes it possible for you to have a wider, more diversified assortment of avocational interests.

You need a broad assortment of interests for your physical and mental health and for your social adaptability. Try adding at least one new interest each year if you want to keep alive and growing. There is no end to the variety of possibilities to explore.

There are the things you make almost "from scratch":

Dottie makes delectable fudge.
Ada is tops in knitting.
Anna weaves the homiest rugs.
Martha quilts the loveliest quilts.
Louise crochets one neat afghan after another.

There are the things you do out of doors:

Fay spends hours bird watching.

Margaret hikes long miles on mountain trails.

Pearl spends many evenings studying the stars.

Mary grows armloads of gorgeous roses.

Virginia hunts the open spaces on her horse and saddle.

There are the things you delight in collecting:

Gladys collects postmarks.

Irene collects bells.

Ruth collects pitchers.

Clarene collects pottery.

Harriet collects rare specimens of wood.

Edna collects organ music records.

And then:

Janet refinishes small pieces of furniture.

Miriam does exciting things in photography.

Sadie "lets go" in creative writing.

Grace haunts ancient cemeteries for rare bits of historical information.

Lois corresponds with people in many lands.

Doris specializes in flower arrangement.

Coralee relaxes with her violin.

Travel, concerts, reading — what do you enjoy? What do you do, and what are you learning to do? Whatever you do, keep alive and growing.

We were traveling by car between Nairobi, Kenya, and Musoma, Tanzania. Laura was traveling with us. She was a "retired" schoolteacher from the States who had come to Mogadiscio, Somalia, to teach in the American School. Since it was her vacation time she was traveling to see friends in other countries. At all times she carried with her a notebook and pencil. The name of a plant, the elevation of a mountain, the customs of a tribe, the preparation of a food, the color and appearance of a bird, the distance between two significant points, the temperature at the equator, and a multitude of other details caught her attention and were captured in that little book. She reminded me of an enthusiastic, energetic young woman just entering the teaching career. I observed her a number of days and concluded that her "aliveness" would keep her happy, interesting, and helpful till the close of her life.

Every human being needs to be serving God and his fellowmen if he is to experience a sense of wholeness and be saved from a sense of utter futility. For the Christian, service is at once a response of thanks and devotion to God, and the saving of one's self. " . . . whosoever will lose his life for my sake, the same shall save it" (Luke 9:24b).

The single woman needs to make a special effort to be serving others rather than to be primarily serving herself. For the woman whose vocation is primarily one of serving the Lord through such activities as healing, or teaching, or other phases of social service, the need for an avocational service experience will likely not be as great as for the woman who has some routine occupation in which she has little or no opportunity for significant personal contact with others.

For you who are represented by this latter person, many of the avocational interests such as those listed above have in them not only the possibility of making you a more versatile person, thereby increasing your effectiveness in many ways; they have in them also the potential for being of service to others.

The person who loves to knit can find literally millions of people who need warm clothing. The person who finds it relaxing to cook tasty foods in her kitchen after a day in the office can always learn of some aged couple or ill mother who needs some food. The woman who relaxes with a musical instrument must surely know persons who need the cheer it could bring to them.

Really, many women not only find ways of serving through their recreational interests; they also discover that the activities entered with service motivation become a genuine recreation experience for them in themselves. There are simple, individual ways of serving that abound all around us. They are so obvious that I will not enumerate them. There are the organized community avenues of service like functioning on auxiliaries of hospitals or other institutions, or giving time to the day care centers for the mentally retarded.

And there are the avenues of service provided by the church: missionary circles, teaching opportunities, youth leadership, and many others. A few years ago, I did some research to discover the degree of involvement of a group of over one hundred single women in service activities provided by the church. The extent and quality of the service they were performing was excitingly significant in the life of the church as well as in their own lives. Don't miss this opportunity.

I know that many times there are circumstances which determine our work and living location or our church home or our living arrangements. A specific vocational opportunity which is challenging to us may take us to a location where social possibilities are limited or church relationships are not ideal.

But some of you are mobile enough that you can do a great deal of choosing and determining what sort of circumstances you will settle into. As much as possible you should give careful consideration to the various facets that hold significance for your well-being before you make a longtime commitment to an area.

Think carefully not only of vocational opportunities and salaries but also of the possibilities for satisfactory living arrangements, stimulating social relationships, and congenial church affiliation. You should be reasonably assured that in each of these areas there is potential to meet your needs.

Speaking of church affiliation: you may be interested to know that small congregations seem to offer the most satisfying atmosphere and fellowship for many single women. Here every person counts regardless of marriage status. There is need for everyone to be involved in the life and service of the congregation. Social and fellowship activities more frequently cut across lines of age and sex so that there is much more of a family mood present.

The single girl must also plan for her senior years. Whereas the married woman can usually look toward retirement years in terms of her husband's income and their joint provision for the declining years, the single woman needs to take the initiative and do her own creative planning. Some women are tempted to procrastinate in this area. They have just themselves to provide for, they think, and they feel selfish if they save or invest for themselves when there are cries of need on every hand. Often their best earning years are past before it dawns on them that they had better do some very careful planning lest they become someone else's financial responsibility and that therefore taking care of their future may be a form of unselfishness rather than of selfishness.

Because of diversity of circumstances that surrounds each one of you, it is impossible for me to include significant specific financial advice. Rather, I would counsel you to seek an understanding, well-informed person to look at your financial situation with you and project plans for the years ahead. While our temporal "securities" are really quite insecure, we do not neglect meeting our responsibilities just because we may not live to reap the benefits.

# 7

## Single Life by the Decade

Social scientists discuss a woman's life in terms of her involvement in the family. They say she is born, starts school at six, enters teens at thirteen, marries at twenty, bears children until age twenty-six, rears children until age forty-six, launches her family, spends middle age in the empty nest with her spouse, and finally spends a number of aging years as a widow. [8] Then each period is studied separately. The developmental tasks common to that period are considered. By tasks we mean the growth responsibilities the individual assumes for his development as he relates himself to his life situation. [9]

When the single woman begins to view her life as a whole, she follows this outline of a woman's life until she reaches later adolescence. Then she drops into oblivion, for she does not belong in the categories that follow and the developmental tasks described for women usually do not apply to her.

For some time I have had an urge to push all the married women off the outline just beyond adolescence and keep the single women on the line and see what the periods of their lives are like. The same benefits of understanding which married people gain through studying the "normal" life cycle may be available to single women as they take a comprehensive view of the single life.

But is there really a pattern that single women follow through the years? I believe there is. It may not be as clearly marked as is the pattern of those who are married, but it is there. Since the markings are less clear, it may be helpful to think of the single life by the decade. Try to discern what is typical during each decade of life. Decades are arbitrary periods and are suggestive guides, rather than final dividers of one phase of life from another. For this reason you should not be troubled if you find your experiences lagging behind or running ahead of the decade being described.

What I share with you in this comprehensive view will not be the exact experience of any

---

8. Evelyn Millis Duvall, *Family Development* (New York: J. B. Lippincott Company, 1967), pp. 14, 15.
9. *Ibid.*, p. 37.

one of you. But you will likely find yourself moving on and off the scene as it is presented. It is more nearly the composite pattern of many women. In this sense it serves as a sort of summary of much of the material in the earlier chapters.

## *Twenty to thirty.*

This decade is characterized by indefiniteness and general insecurity. This is the time when you and your family need to discover and accept your status.

You have undoubtedly asked yourself dozens of times, "Will I — will I not marry?" You have wondered, "Shall I claim to be one of the older members of the youth group or shall I say that I'm one of the younger single women? When do I leave the one camp and enter the other?"

Many women have the tendency to cling to the notion that they are still among the youthful ones. They try to bolster this claim by making friends in the younger set. This is very understandable because society places a premium on youth, especially for unmarrieds. Then, too, most of their friends of their age have married and are engaged in their own different world of activities.

Finally near the close of the decade it dawns on you that you are undeniably a single woman by status. Then you have the task of accepting the status, taking it positively, discovering what it really means and how it can be most productive and satisfying. Many women find this a very difficult task because their early conditioning toward singleness has been negative and their former goal of marriage has been frustrated.

While positive acceptance of singleness comes before age thirty for many women, many others keep postponing it and many never do achieve it.

When finally the woman in this decade accepts her status as a single woman, she has then to discover what is the role of the single woman. What is she supposed to be and to do? How is she to fit into her culture? What is her place in the church?

While her married sister has had much assistance to understand the role that is hers, very little help of any kind has been given to the single woman. So she has to try as best she can to discover her role and accept or modify it.

Some single women have chosen a vocation or career already in their teens. But many other women have taken only stopgap jobs in their teens expecting that they would be married in their early twenties. Now what shall they do? Shall they take time out for college or for some other specialized training at this late date? Or shall they just keep plodding away where they are? In other words, what shall they do with a life, the plans for which have not materialized?

There is usually a radical change in the social milieu — the friendship group and activities — in this decade. The majority of your girl friends have married by twenty-two or twenty-three. They are still your friends, but the friendship isn't the same! They have been building trousseaus and layettes and after oh-ing and ah-ing about so many of them, you are ready to find friends with common interests or experiences. And the men? By mid-twenties most of them have settled down with your girl friends. Those who haven't married have gone overseas or found some other adventurous occupation.

This is for many women a decade of spiritual crisis. It may have in it spiritual testing, flux, reorganizing, revitalizing, upheaval, and/or maturing. While the experience varies greatly from woman to woman, it is usually highly significant. The multiple developmental tasks we've been discussing are faith-shaking to some women. They question the leading of the Lord, the goodness of God, and the importance of Christian morality. Other women face this multiplicity of tasks and instead of having their faith shaken they engage their spiritual resources for positive attitudes and action as they move through these experiences. They become spiritually strong and vital in the midst of them.

In general the 20-30 decade is a period of both great liability and great possibility. Failure to negotiate the tasks enumerated may find a woman at the close of this period very lonely, insecure vocationally, immature socially, and spiritually at sea. Too often she is full of bitterness, restlessness, and resentment. But if she has accomplished these tasks one by one, even though the going has been rough, she may be able to close the one decade and step into the next with head erect, with confidence, with a sense of purpose and meaning, with faith in God, and with a minimum of scars.

### *Thirty to forty.*

Professional development tends to characterize this decade. Even the woman who chose a profession in her late teens or early twenties will by now have the feeling that since her vocation is the big thing in her life, she wants to expand or deepen it. Perhaps she will enter a new phase of it. She may go to workshops or conventions set up for her professional interest. She may join an organization that will give her new insights and keep her up-to-date. She will read about it and talk with more experienced people about it. In other words, she will go into depth in her profession or vocation.

For many women the 30-40 decade is marked by a surge of avocational development also. There are some women who for particular reasons, or sets of circumstances, were unable to become involved in a vocation that holds challenge to them in that 20-30 period. They feel sort of stuck for life with a job that is mundane and uninteresting. For them especially this may be the period of avocational development, of taking on the creative, enriching, stimulating activities that make life worth living. Even the women who enjoy their work very much are likely to find by this decade that they need to be expanding their interests and doing something more than their work.

Stabilizing of living arrangements marks this decade for many women. Very few single women settle down to a stable or "permanent" living arrangement under thirty. Along with the many adjustments of that 20-30 decade is usually or frequently a mobility that reaches over into the thirties. But the fun of moving around and going places all the time wanes a bit as the years roll by. Sometime in the thirties the urge for stability increases. By this time many women want to settle down in some place of their own. They want their possessions around them. They want to be independent and be themselves. They want to express their own creativity and domestic interests. So they begin to make decisions and work toward the goal of having their own home.

Again this decade holds its share of liabilities and possible assets. On the negative side, the battle of loneliness is not won once for all in the 20-30 period. It can become very acute in the 30-40 decade when most of a woman's peers and brothers and sisters are deeply involved in rearing their families. While the women are talking easily about diapering their babies or about the bald spot appearing on the husband's head, the single woman in their midst is gripped suddenly with a deep sense of aloneness. This can happen to her quite some time after she thought she had overcome her loneliness.

The battle with selfishness becomes especially fierce at this time for many women. "Why not do the things we like to do in the way we like to do them?" they say. And since they are in a position where they can pretty well do this many women succumb to deep patterns of selfish living that carry through the years.

Biological needs and drives become quite intense for many women during this period. If within the same person there is the combination of loneliness, self-pity, and deep biological-sexual needs, there is almost certain to be temptation to illicit male relationships.

But on the positive side, during these years there is also the possibility of professional advancement, of creative discoveries, of developing new and varied friendships, of discovering the joy of living for others, and of finding satisfaction in the everyday experiences of life.

*Forty to fifty.*

What happens in this decade? The group of tasks to be accomplished is not as distinct as in the earlier decades. We see this period more in terms of its characteristics.

For some women these years may become a drag. There is little new and challenging in them, just more of the same humdrum. They feel life ended at forty instead of having begun there. If their maternal drives have been strong, the coming of menopause may be a very crucial time to them. The finality of it may be difficult for them to cope with. They see their brothers and sisters involved in the weddings of their children and the joys of their grandchildren. They see their own lives as barren and empty and so must struggle with the problems of how to keep alive and how to find meaning in life.

But for other women these are the comfortable, relatively quiet years. They are no longer restless and they have stopped roaming about. They are more relaxed and more efficient in their vocational duties. They are now living fully the life they spent years preparing to live.

In this decade many single women need to establish a new relationship with aging parents. They need to decide to what extent they should assume responsibility for them. The answer to this problem frequently means a rather major disruption of one sort or another in the woman's living arrangements for a period of time.

## *Fifty to sixty.*

Some people feel the 50-60 decade is so similar to the 40-50 span that it hardly merits separate recognition. Perhaps it is marked chiefly by an intensifying of whatever the characteristics of the 40-50 decade have been.

Certainly it is a time when there are many more careful thoughts about the future. Thoughts about financial security, thoughts about living arrangements in the years ahead, thoughts about activities and ways of being useful beyond retirement — all of these become increasingly significant. Careful preparation for the future may be the most important new task to be accomplished in this decade.

In this period many women begin to have anxieties about what it will be like to age alone without a family around them. Still others face the fear of being pushed out of the stream of usefulness by the onrush of fortune-seeking youth long before their productivity is actually depleted.

But for still others whose plans for retirement are well established there is something of an eagerness for the time when the demands of life will no longer be so exacting.

## *Sixty to seventy and beyond.*

So much depends on foundations laid in early

decades as to what happens now. This is the decade of retirement for most employed women! Change is difficult by now and yet there is change on every hand. Activities change. In many instances living arrangements and location change and along with this comes the change of friends and associates.

Here perhaps, more than at any time, the lack of a family — loving husband, strong sons, gentle daughters, and affectionate grandchildren — is felt. There is loneliness in the look ahead. One of my single friends told me that she comes nearest resenting being single when she reads the obituaries of single women and feels the aloneness they portray.

But for many women this is the period of relaxed activity. It is the time of living more fully for others and of keeping aware of the progress of the church of God. It is the day of deepened faith and new levels of trust, of long hours for meditation and prayer. It is a period of retrospect when many of the pieces of a lifetime seem to fall into place and make sense. It is now that many of life's early questions lose their importance in the light of the meaningfulness of what has been. A lovely, elderly friend of mine wrote recently,

"I have been happy in my single state, happy to have had some part in the Lord's work. I do not believe that the fault was mine or my parents' that God could not use me as a married woman. I was His; He led me; He enabled me. I made mistakes; I did not follow as closely as I could have, but I was His. I believe with all my heart that I could serve God better single than married. And if it had not been so, I would have had a husband. So as God's child I am happy in my single state in which I find myself at seventy-two years of age."

For the woman of God this final period is one of renewed excitement and anticipation. In today's terms it is "the greatest"! She anticipates permanent fellowship with the Lord. She waits to exchange her failing body for her glorious immortal body. She looks forward to being in the state in which marriage and family are superseded by membership in God's family. And finally she delights in the prospect of the unfathomable joys of eternal life.

# 8

## Finally

You can live well. I have tried to provide insights and guides that will be of value to you in your effort to live life at its best. It is really not so much a matter of being married or of being single as it is of learning to live well and doing that in whichever state you are called to live.

So keep your sense of humor functioning, your love and understanding of others growing, and your fellowship with God deepening, and the good life is for you.

And if you have learned to live well as a single woman, you will have done your part to break the undesirable, often unwarranted stereotype of the single woman for the generation that follows you.

I have written to you as single women. Many of you will always be single women. Some of you will marry. If you have learned to live well as single women, you will have a wealth of experience and understanding to take into your marriage for its enrichment.

If you do marry, have the good common sense not to be smug about it as though you have now arrived and your single friends have been left behind.

On the other hand, do not be too surprised if some of your single friends reject you temporarily when you have had no feelings of rejecting them. Have patience with them until they regain their poise. After all, they have a great deal of adjusting to do in order to accept you in this new role. If you give them time, most of them will get around to loving you again!

# BIBLIOGRAPHY

Acrea, Jeannette. "Happy Though Single," *Psychology for Living*, Vol. V, No. 1 (January 1963). An article in which a Christian psychologist speaks to the problems of sexual need in the life of the unmarried Christian woman.

Brown, Helen Gurley. *Sex and the Single Girl*. New York: Random House, Distributors (Published by Bernard Geis Associates), 1962. A startling disclosure of current exploitation of women's basic needs. The author gives a pagan treatment of the single woman's life, relating most areas of her existence to illicit sex behavior.

Capper, Melville, and William H. Morgan. *Toward Christian Marriage*. Chicago 10: Inter-Varsity Press, 1958. A treatment of sex and marriage as God intends them for the Christian. Some attention is given to the needs of the unmarried.

Cummings, Gwen. *The Single Girl's Guide to Living in the City*. New York: Association Press, 1968. A book for younger unmarried women which deals with many of the problems they face upon going to the large city to live and work.

Dunn, David. *Try Giving Yourself Away*. Scarsdale, N.Y.: The Updegraff Press, Ltd., 1947. A book that is chock-full of homespun philosophy of happiness! It introduces all kinds of simple things one can do to achieve happiness by helping others "without pay."

Duvall, Evelyn Millis. *Family Development*. New

York: J. B. Lippincott, 1967. "The thesis of the book is that families grow through predictable stages of development that can be understood in terms of the development of the individual family members and of the family-as-a-whole."

Havemann, Ernest, and Patricia Salter West. *They Went to College.* New York: Harcourt, Brace and Company, 1952. A study of the American College graduate which includes statistics and findings on the "Ubiquitous Spinster."

Hillyard, Marion. *A Woman Doctor Looks at Life and Love.* New York: Doubleday and Company, Inc., 1957. A single woman doctor who practiced in obstetrics and gynecology for many years gives advice and help toward self-knowledge to women of all ages, both married and single.

Hugen, M. D. *The Church's Ministry to the Older Unmarried.* Grand Rapids, Mich.: Wm. B. Eerdmans Publishing Company, 1959. A sociological, psychological, and theological study of single adults in the churches. It identifies the difficulties experienced in single living and shows how these may hinder the life of faith. It also defines the church's role in edifying the whole person.

King, Evelyn E. *A Study of the Status of the Unmarried Women Graduates of Eastern Mennonite College.* (Unpublished thesis) 1962. A study of 124 single women graduates of Eastern Mennonite College in which vocational, economic, academic, and social statuses are portrayed.

Miller, Keith. *A Second Touch.* Waco, Tex.: Word Books, 1967. A book for persons trying to live their faith in God, who have become frustrated, lonely, and anxious in trying. A chapter on responsible loving relationships between men and women is especially pertinent.

Name Withheld. "If You Don't Marry," *His Magazine*, Vol. 18, No. 5 (February 1958). A sharing of experiences and insights into the way the single Christian woman relates to her desires for husband, home, and children. Marriage is portrayed as a shadow of the relationship between Christ and His children, the substance of which is available for all who cultivate it.

Narramore, Clyde M. *The Unmarried Girl.* Grand Rapids, Mich.: Zondervan Publishers. Psychology for Living Booklet Number Seventy-two. A pamphlet written from the Christian viewpoint to help unmarried girls appraise their own problems of singlehood and discover resources with which they can be resolved.

Ogg, Elizabeth. *Why Some Women Stay Single.* New York: Public Affairs Pamphlet No. 177. A pamphlet which analyzes the status of single women and provides guidelines to help meet the problems of singleness with positive approaches. It shifts the emphasis on marriage as a status symbol to living creatively in whatever state one lives. No attempt is made to distinguish between Christian and secular goals.

Price, Eugenia. *Woman to Woman.* Grand Rapids, Mich.: Zondervan Publishing House, 1959. Written to show the difference Christ makes in a woman's life, this book speaks specifically

both to the married and to the unmarried woman.
Reed, Ruth. *The Single Woman.* New York: The Macmillan Company, 1942. A positive approach to singleness which portrays the single woman as playing a vital and important role in our society. Reed sees the possibility of a well-rounded existence and a good life for singles.
Resenteur, Phyllis I. *The Single Woman.* New York: The Bobbs-Merrill Company, Inc., 1961. Portrayal of the sophisticated contemporary approach to singleness. It is clearly not an acceptable guide for Christian women.
Seagle, Inez. "No Husband or Anything," *Christian Living*, Seventh Year, Eighth Issue (August 1960). An article contrasting the lives of marrieds and singles and pointing up wholesome alternatives to marriage for singles.
Smith, M. B. *The Single Woman of Today.* New York 16: The Philosophical Library, Inc., 1952. Written to shed light on the psychological and sociological aspects of the status of the single woman.
Stalker, James. *The Trial and Death of Jesus.* Grand Rapids, Mich.: Zondervan Publishing House. A book which describes the closing scenes of Christ's earthly history. Written as a "Devotional History" it comments on many aspects of human relationships.
Steward, Hal D. "It's Time for Society to Discover the Singles," *Daily News Record* (January 1968). A newspaper article reporting on a pilot program designed to help single persons live with their single state in a society structured for couples.

Tournier, Paul. *Escape from Loneliness.* Philadelphia: The Westminster Press, 1958. In this work on man's isolation from man, the author devotes a number of pages to the problems of female celibacy.

Towns, Elmer. *The Single Adult and the Church.* Glendale, Calif.: Regal Books Division G/L Publications, 1967. This book was written to help the church formulate plans to meet the needs of young single adults. It suggests concrete proposals as first steps in the process. It emphasizes the challenge these persons are to the church.

## THE AUTHOR

Evelyn King Mumaw is a native of eastern Pennsylvania but has lived in Virginia since 1946. She was educated at Eastern Mennonite College (BRE), Wheaton College, and Madison College (M.A.Ed.). During the years from 1951 to 1965 she served as Dean of Women at Eastern Mennonite College, Harrisonburg, Va. During her early years in personnel work she became especially interested in the college women who apparently would not marry for some time, if ever. This interest prompted her to do her thesis for a master's degree in 1961 entitled, *A Study of the Status of the Unmarried Women Graduates of Eastern Mennonite College.* This study provided basic material for the addresses, class lectures, counseling, and group discussions regarding single women which have followed.

In June of 1965 she was married to John R. Mumaw who is President Emeritus of Eastern Mennonite College. From August 1965 until June 1966, she and her husband traveled around the world visiting missions in fourteen different countries. Since their return to the States she has assisted her husband in missionary conferences and in conferences on the home in a number of states and has been active in women's work in camps, at retreats, and in her home community. In September 1968, she again accepted responsibility for another term of service as Dean of Women at Eastern Mennonite College.